OPEN UP!

HOW
DO YOU
FEEL?

Guillermo Kahlo, photograph of Frida Kahlo inscribed "*De tu amigo que esta muy triste*" (From your friend who is very sad); tears drawn on by Frida, 1932

HOW DO YOU FEEL?

A SPECTACULAR COMPENDIUM OF IDEAS,

INTERACTIVE GAMES, PROVOCATIONS, TESTS, AND TRICKS

THAT EXPLORE THE WORLD OF WHAT YOU FEEL AND WHY

EDITED BY EDGAR GERRARD HUGHES

FOREWORD BY MARINA WARNER

PRINCETON ARCHITECTURAL PRESS · NEW YORK

Published by
Princeton Architectural Press
202 Warren Street
Hudson, New York 12534
www.papress.com

First published in the UK in 2021 by
Redstone Press as *The Book of Emotions*
7a St Lawrence Terrace
London, UK W10 5SU
www.theredstoneshop.com

Princeton Architectural Press edition © 2021

Texts © Edgar Gerrard Hughes 2021

Foreword © Marina Warner 2021

"From Humours to Interoception: Emotions in
Body and Mind" © Noga Arikha 2021

"Ecstasy" © Jules Evans 2021

"Disgust" © Christopher Turner 2021

"Blushing" © Charles Boyle 2021

"Transmissions from the Unconscious"
© Rose Dempsey 2021

"After the Party" and "Anger is an Energy"
© Natalie Hume 2021

"The 36-Question Love Spell" was originally
published in A. Aron et al., "The Experimental
Generation of Interpersonal Closeness: A
Procedure and Some Preliminary Findings,"
Personality and Social Psychology Bulletin 23,
no. 4 (April 1997).

"Emotional Heat Maps" was originally published in
L. Nummenmaa et al., "Bodily Maps of Emotions,"
*Proceedings of the National Academy of Sciences
in America* 19, no. 6 (December 2013).

ISBN 978-1-61689-968-4
Library of Congress Control Number: 2021932663

For Redstone Press
Design: Julian Rothenstein
Editorial Consultant: Natalie Hume
Artwork: Tom Baxter
Production: Geoff Barlow

For Princeton Architectural Press
Cover design: Paul Wagner

Cover images:
Top: Saul Leiter, *Jean,* c. 1948, © Saul Leiter
Foundation, courtesy Howard Greenberg Gallery
Bottom: Photograph from an advertisement
for Melhuish's New Harvest Flour, c. 1932,
courtesy Wellcome Images

An adaptation of Robert Plutchik's wheel of emotions

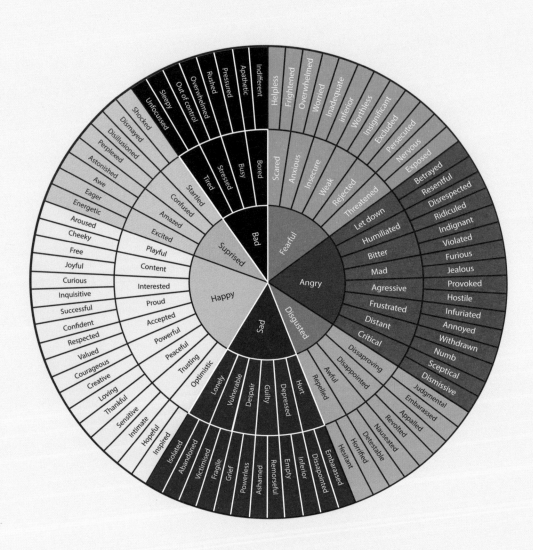

CONTENTS

FOREWORD BY MARINA WARNER

Those flimsy cellophane Chinese fish, which you lay on the palm of a friend's hand to find out how passionate she is, provoke much oohing and aahing when the translucent sliver flops belly up or curls so vigorously it jumps off altogether. It's only a game, and it makes everyone laugh, but if the answer comes that you're boiling over with a raging heat of desire or, worse, that you're a cold fish, it does give you pause. In *How Do You Feel?*, the editor Edgar Gerrard Hughes has amassed a wealth of evidence about many attempts across time, serious approaches as well as playful devices, to find answers to the question "How do you feel?"

Emotions can be events: a rush of anger, a loss that wreaks terrible grief, or sudden joy. But they are also states, moods, a characteristic temperament or disposition: panickiness, sadness, ennui. Some remain wide and vague, suggestive and indefinable. "Moodiness" feels emotional enough, but what emotion is it? Indefinability may be central to the power of other feelings: Spanish *duende* as expressed by the flamenco dancer, Portuguese *saudade* as embodied in the voice of the fado singer. Where emotions come from and how to name them keep the cognitive scientists and philosophers hard at work; novelists, poets, dramatists try to seize the feelings as they happen, and we judge writers by their success in achieving nuance and shade; psychologists and quiz masters create test sheets—both in earnest and in jest.

The metaphors used to describe the passions—the word "emotion" only emerges in English in the seventeenth century—borrow from different grounds of experience and draw on changing models of human nature. In classical times, divine powers acted as daimonic external forces, erupting in human lives, visiting upon them unwanted desires and drives: Eris is the goddess of strife who incites the jealous rivalry among the goddesses that ultimately brings about the fall of Troy; Venus callously lights the fire that consumes Dido with love for Aeneas and destroys her.

Another legacy from the classics, the theory of the humors, discussed here by Noga Arikha on pp. 34–36, dominated medical knowledge for over a millennium and led to the construction of an intricate system of correspondences to explain human characteristics; different emotional types—choleric, phlegmatic, melancholic, sanguine, etc.—were fitted to a model of "as above so below," a continuum joining up the far distant stars and planets to a particular person's organs and determining their personality. To be born under the sign of Saturn made you prone to an excess of black bile—and consequently to suffer the ravages of the black dog of melancholy, or what today would be called depression (see p. 127). This "microcosm–macrocosm" model was the rationale for horoscopes, still believed by many to play a part in our character and destiny. The most learned minds of the Renaissance trusted this knowledge: Marsilio Ficino, the first translator of Plato from Greek into Latin, would play his viol in moonlight to the planet Venus, in hope of exciting her erotic essence to descend and irradiate him.

The contributors to this collection show again and again how a bright theory will grow dim after a certain time but that traces of the superseded system linger long and influentially. In my Catholic childhood, emotions were sins, all tangled up with various failures and transgressions, spiritual and social. "Forgive me, Father, for I have sinned," I would begin my confession. "I had bad thoughts about X, I wished her dead." "I lost my temper with so-and-so." "I've been lazy and didn't try at hockey." And so forth. Such dreaded sinful feelings might have arisen from natural inborn traits, personal, ineradicable predilections, and these in turn became twisted up with emotions: Greed (one of the Deadly Sins) could lead to what William Blake hymned "the lineaments of gratified desire," and then to agonies of guilt and shame. Likewise, Vanity or Pride may produce delightful states of self-satisfaction—followed by a fall.

Some of these ancient Christian vices still exist but have changed value: anger, shading into indignation and outrage, is now often upheld as a virtue and a strength (a subject explored by Natalie Hume on pp. 144–45); lust, too, considered as Eros or the life force, no longer seems only the devil's business. Mendacity and fraud are still publicly disclaimed but are practiced with smug impunity in public life (lying and deceiving are not exactly emotions, though the self-belief that buoys them is a perverse variety of self-love). Acedia (listlessness, a kind of torpor of the soul) was accounted the eighth Deadly Sin in the Middle Ages. It's one of the "lost" feelings retrieved here on p. 122, but it corresponds to the widespread state of disorientation and lack of motivation that the pandemic has inflicted on so many.

Powerful emotions may also spring from social lapses and the ensuing public shame that inspires far more intense feelings than any sense of sinfulness. At my English boarding school, my new classmates baffled me with their stinging talk of "vim." I would learn later that the word comes from the Latin *vis* (force or energy); they would also say, impatiently, "Show some gumption!" (The latter is a Scottish word for common sense, according to the dictionary.) In themselves vim and gumption weren't exactly emotions, but in my memories, they're emotionally tangled up with winning the approval of others; lacking them led to ignominy, the sheer emotional misery of social failure.

However, just as the humors aren't given much credence today, the same goes for some of the Enlightenment's rationalist approaches to defining the emotions. A satirist proposed a "female thermometer" to measure a woman's degree of passion, and, in the enthusiasm for objectivity, for measurements, tables, and charts, such an instrument might well have been popular. Taxonomies were drawn up to try and pin down all the slippery vagaries of human emotions: Franz Xaver Messerschmidt's sculptured grimaces, leers, frowns, and guffaws are among the startling results of the Age of Reason (pp. 54–57). These endeavors were later accompanied by the craze for phrenology— deducing someone's tendencies from the bumps on their skull—and for drawing up portrait galleries of probable wrongdoers. Evil propensities were identifiable, it was claimed, from certain features. Beauty spots or wrinkles on foreheads were mapped to reveal character, and these diagnostic fantasies were in turn applied to the emotions: a tendency to rage, discernible in the set of a man's chin, could portend he would likely commit murder.

The cult of "sentiment" set up a counterweight to these severe applications of reason, and fine feelings or "sensibility" became an important element in civility. The sometimes lachrymose effects of the rise in sensitivity were much explored—and parodied—in the first modern novels, as in Jane Austen's *Sense and Sensibility*. But the change of attitude had benign results: for example, an earlier taste for acts of mockery and "cozening," leading to the merriment of the japesters and the humiliation of their targets (such as the scene of Malvolio's comeuppance in Shakespeare's *Twelfth Night*), ceased to excite the same degree of callous enthusiasm. Ideas of *Einfühlung*, eventually translated into English as "empathy" in 1909, began to win strong ethical approval.

Romanticism then intensified commitment to the emotions as a moral good—and a useful compass. In a letter of 1817 to his brother, the poet John Keats famously introduced the concept of "Negative Capability…when man is capable of being in uncertainties, mysteries, doubts, without any irritable reaching after fact and reason." For Keats this state of absorptive passivity was primarily connected to inspiration; his words have provoked much puzzled reflection, but this notion has since become closely connected to withstanding difficulties—to what has come to be called "resilience." The writer Michèle Roberts, in her perceptive memoir called *Negative Capability: A Diary of a Difficult Year* (2020), describes how she adopted Keats's principle, allowing everything that life threw at her to happen without worrying about finding an explanation. In her account, emotion becomes part of her conscious practice and an effective mode of survival. Her strategy resonates with the passage from George Eliot's *Daniel Deronda* (1876) when Deronda tells Gwendolen, "Take your fear as a safeguard. It is like quickness of hearing. It may make consequences passionately present to you. *Try and take hold of your sensibility, and use it as if it were a faculty, like vision*" (my emphasis). Gwendolen's emotional disarray, after her husband has drowned and she feels herself implicated in his death, can be shaped into a faculty she can sharpen and use.

Once we enter the modern period and the contemporary world, the search to understand human emotions turns more and more toward a subject's interiority, to the psyche and its traumas. Theories of psychology and most especially psychoanalysis predominate. Taking the pulse of emotions leads to concepts of consciousness itself, "the feeling of what happens," as Antonio Damasio termed it, and attempts at defining the emotions become again and again a fascinating quest to account for human nature itself.

The section about lost and found emotions on pp. 121–35, a wonderfully rich glossary of unfamiliar terms from all over the world, shows how language can take a lead in shaping experience: "Yes, I've felt that," you say to yourself, "but I didn't have a word for it." It is not just that emotions form the landscape of consciousness but that they bring subtle facets of consciousness into relief, like a map that takes note of features that were always there but never before remarked. The word "gigil"—wanting to gobble up a baby in delight at her sweet chubbiness— strikes me as deliciously onomatopoeic for that strange desire that comes over one. Reading this section made me wonder all over again about the Wittgensteinian maxim that "the limits of my language are the limits of my world."

So far in this introduction I've been using "emotions," "passions," and "feelings" interchangeably, but they aren't identical: feelings can be sensations, and their emotional component weak: to be hot or cold can result from desire or terror, but not necessarily. Emotion implies a sentient subject, but models of agency, consciousness, and our attendant emotions tend to suffer from long time lags, as the metaphors keep being carried on the flux of poetry, songs, and fiction, long after the theories of the scientists and psychologists have moved on. For most of the twentieth century, imagery of the nervous system and electromagnetism prevailed: in the sixties, my mother would say of a friend that she was "very highly strung." Now, the tension tends more to the architectonic—"stressed"—or hydraulic—"best not to keep it all bottled up." Current approaches tend to cast the individual as an integer, unique and autonomous, with emotions deep inside and harmfully repressed. This understanding dominates in the age when self-exposure (autofiction, selfies) enjoys high popularity, even though social media are making space for atavistic rage and malice, and spurring on more recently identified emotions such as sadism (pleasure in another's pain), voyeurism (pleasure in intruding and peeping) and FOMO (the fear of missing out, as described on p. 127). The need for countervailing feelings has become urgent, and a new emphasis on mitigating states has been rising fast: empathy motivates kindness, and kindness, like altruism, can be a deep source of happiness for everyone involved. The word is related to "kin" and "kindred," and acts of kindness establish fellow feeling. To be kind, to pursue the ideals of "promiscuous care" are paths to well-being. Yet kindness isn't an emotion, strictly speaking It would be more accurate to say that kindness, like Keats's negative capability, is a state of mind that perceives emotions as a stimulus and response combined, formed between the giver and the receiver. The pulse may quicken with pleasure and tears even well during an act of kindness—as many of us have been fortunate to experience with neighbors during lockdown. In their book *On Kindness*, Adam Phillips and Barbara Taylor write, "Kindness's original meaning of kinship or sameness has stretched over time to encompass sentiments that today go by a wide variety of names—sympathy, generosity, altruism, benevolence, humanity, compassion, pity, empathy....The precise meanings of these words vary, but fundamentally they all denote what the Victorians called 'open-heartedness,' the sympathetic expansiveness linking self to other."

In many cultures, narratives of the self extend beyond the borders of the solitary psyche: theories of reincarnation hold that past existences will affect you in your latest sojourn. Many of the puzzles that inspired psychic research in the nineteenth century still remain. Teresa Brennan, in an interesting book, *The Transmission of Affect* (2004), asked, "What does it mean when you say you felt the mood in the room?" One of the features of isolation under the coronavirus has been the curious deadness of the Zoom space: it does not allow that feeling for what others are feeling to be communicated. Affect, as in Brennan's title, has become, alongside empathy, a dominant term in the understanding of emotions today, interestingly accepting an intrinsic reciprocity of exchange. Empathy, and being capable of affect, enlarges on the older, deep-rooted ideas of sensibility and sympathy, but whereas sympathy is personal, empathy includes nonpersonal relationships: you can have empathy for someone you do not know, and maybe the capacity to feel for such a person or persons presents a test of humanity in the first place.

Jules Evans, writing about ecstasy on pp. 156–59, comments that a desire for shared experiences motivated the Victorians' table-turning. They were scientifically minded and conducted elaborate controlled experiments in telepathy and premonition and dream interpretation; this was a way of escaping the tepid humdrum, he suggests, reaching an altered state—a communal high. Yet the phenomenon of collective emotions raises the question of sincerity: these feelings are often sparked in contact with others who may be strangers—choking up at a funeral even when you weren't close to the dead person, growing teary at a royal wedding on television, or experiencing euphoria in political rallies or evangelical rituals. The quest for extreme states of emotion, culminating in the loss of self or nirvana—Jim Morrison's call to "break on through to the other side"—has been attempted always and everywhere, by various means. We even learn here that, as the song goes, animals in the sea do it (dolphins preying on puffer fish!).

After reveling in the kaleidoscopic array of ideas in *How Do You Feel?*, we could see literature itself as a quest, generation after generation, to map the psyche and its passions; this unfinished business keeps us fascinated—by Phaedra's frenzy of love, by the longings of the doomed Keats, by the vibrating, quivering responses of Virginia Woolf's cast of characters in *The Waves* (caught in a mesh of intervibrating frequencies), and by the stark despair of Sylvia Plath.

"We go to poetry to be forwarded in ourselves," wrote Seamus Heaney. But, even more passionately, we go to literature and music and art to learn what our feelings are, to name them so that we can learn more about how you, I, we feel. Edgar Gerrard Hughes has assembled one fresh attempt after another to gain insight into our tumultuous feelings. The images and texts collected here, varied and sparkling as they are, amount to a history of superseded knowledge, of false turnings and dead ends. Being alive now, we can't escape our cultural frame, and the most recent accounts of emotions will inevitably strike you and me as the most persuasive. But can we be sure of this, that our present understanding is now correct and will endure in ways that few of our precursors' theories managed? Kentish Town, London, December 2020

FURTHER READING

Arikha, Noga. *Passions and Tempers: A History of the Humors*. New York: Ecco Press, 2007.

Brennan, Teresa. *The Transmission of Affect*. Ithaca, NY: Cornell University Press, 2004.

The Care Collective (Lynne Segal et al.). *The Care Manifesto*. London: Verso, 2020.

Castle, Terry. *The Female Thermometer: Eighteenth-Century Culture and the Invention of the Uncanny*. New York: Oxford University Press, 1995.

Damasio, Antonio. *The Feeling of What Happens: Body and Emotion in the Making of Consciousness*. Boston: Mariner, 2000.

Eliot, George. *Daniel Deronda*. Edited by Terence Cave. London: Penguin, 1996.

King, Catherine, Mark Tucker, Mark Rylance, and the Marini Consort. *Secrets of the Heavens: Seven Invocations for the Contemplation of Things Celestial*. RiverRun Records, compact disc, 2009.

Phillips, Adam, and Barbara Taylor. *On Kindness*. London: Penguin, 2009.

Roberts, Michèle. *Negative Capability: A Diary of Surviving*. London: Sandstone, 2020.

Warner, Marina. *Phantasmagoria: Spirit Visions, Metaphors, and Media into the Twenty-First Century*. Oxford: Oxford University Press, 2008.

INTRODUCTION: WHAT IS AN EMOTION?

A quivering in the pit of your belly. A scarcely contained surging sensation spreading outward from your heart to your toes. A vague, menacing presence in the depths of your consciousness. Or the deeper conviction, buried somewhere far below the shifting sands of mood, that everything is fine—or not.

When somebody seems incapable of feeling, we say they are "dead inside." But for something so powerful and fundamental, emotion is a slippery concept. Is hope an emotion, for instance? What about curiosity? Thoughtfulness? Aggression? Concentration? Is every experience an emotion? Or is the concept of emotion too vague and multivalent to be of real use?

Feeling body, judging mind?

When we feel something, we are "moved" or "transported." Emotion is motion: the two words share the same French and Latin root. And that makes a lot of sense. If you think of a time when you felt a strong emotion, you will likely recall a sensation of bodily turbulence: butterflies in the stomach, a trembling heart, dry mouth, a sinking feeling, a sudden impulse to pace the room. William James, often identified as the founder of modern psychology, believed that emotion was nothing more nor less than the mind's awareness of bodily disturbance. Weak knees and a pulsing heart are not telltale symptoms of fear, he thought, but fear itself: "A disembodied human emotion is a nonentity."

We often think about emotions in the "language of physics," as the Victorian psychiatrist Henry Maudsley put it: "bright or gloomy, warm or cool, flutter, flurry, tremor, palpitation, cutting, piercing, sweet, bitter, caustic, thrilling, quivering, electric, and so on." Emotions are often framed using what Robert Solomon has termed the "hydraulic metaphor," liable to bubble up, boil over or burst out: like a steam engine in which pressure is constantly building, the gasket will blow if we don't "keep a lid on it."

Such imagery suggests that to feel an emotion is to become aware of the whir of internal machinery to which we are usually—and perhaps preferably—oblivious. Our heart is always keeping time, but we only feel it beating when something has happened to unsettle us. Our stomach is constantly churning food into fuel, but for the most part we'd rather not be too aware of the process.

David Shrigley, *Try to Understand Your Emotions*, 2020

Given this conception of emotions in opposition to the will, it can be tempting to think of them as a sort of enemy within, constantly working to sabotage our better judgment. In Darwinian terms, emotions—especially those that feel particularly primal, such as anger, fear, and disgust—have often been understood as the vestige of an earlier stage of evolution, a troublesome remnant from prehuman ancestors who relied on instinct rather than reason. Taking this to extremes, it is even possible to see all of human history as a war of attrition to impose rational order on the fluctuations of brute feeling. "Domination of human nature," wrote the Dutch historian Johan Huizinga, "can only mean the domination of every man by himself." Even though this might require effort and self-sacrifice, it is ultimately necessary in the name of order and progress. As Alfred Tennyson, fascinated and shaken by his encounter with evolutionary theories, wrote: "Move upward, working out the beast, and let the ape and tiger die."

To those of a more romantic sensibility, on the other hand, the apparent "naturalness" of emotions is exactly what makes them vital: our feelings are our only reliable guides to what is authentic and good: "follow your heart," as the saying goes. Or as Johann Wolfgang von Goethe put it (speaking through his tragic hero Werther), "I am proud of my heart alone, it is the sole source of everything, all our strength, happiness and misery. All the knowledge I possess everyone else can acquire, but my heart is all my own."

For George Eliot, emotion is an irresistible force: "Human feeling is like the mighty rivers that bless the earth: it does not wait for beauty—it flows with resistless force and brings beauty with it." But the notion that passions should be the guide for our reasoning minds rather than its internal opponents was also a key part of the philosophy of David Hume, one of the most famously pragmatic, down-to-earth philosophers in the Western tradition. Reason can help us chart the course, Hume thought, but it can't determine what the destination ought to be. Only pleasure or pain—or the anticipation of pleasure or pain—can direct the rational mind. "Reason is, and ought only to be the slave of the passions," he wrote, "and can never pretend to any other office than to serve and obey them."

Thinking, with feeling

Whether emotion is construed as a troublesome intruder into our ordered mind or as a light to guide our actions, all of the perspectives mentioned above have one thing in common: in each case emotion is identified with the body and as distinct from rational judgment and knowledge. An alternative perspective, with a long legacy of its own, is that emotions are the product of judgment and thought. What if, instead of something that happens to us, emotions are created in our brains, the fruits of complicated moral and intellectual judgments? "A tear is an intellectual thing," as William Blake wrote.

When you're "in the grip" of rage, it doesn't usually feel as though you are making measured calculations. But even apparently uncontrollable anger—or sorrow, or love—often involves the deployment of a lot of complicated judgments. When you lose it with a stranger who's cut into a queue, you are bringing to bear ideas about fairness, the social norms of queuing, and perhaps also the practical effect that your anger might have—for instance, inducing in them the emotion of shame, so that they apologise and take their rightful place at the back of the line.

The psychologist Lisa Feldman Barrett is one of the leading voices for the theory that emotions are "psychologically constructed." Emotions aren't straightforward biological facts, she says, but interpretations that we impose on the bundle of sensations, perceptions, thoughts, and bodily stimulations that we experience in a constant, messy stream. Is your throbbing heartbeat a symptom of fear? Anxiety? Excitement? Does it come from a judgment that your boss is being unreasonable or your own inability to respond calmly to criticism? Or did you just overdo it on the coffee this morning? Our shifting, amorphous feelings coalesce into discrete emotions only when we give them a name and a narrative: "An emotion is your brain's creation of what your bodily sensations mean."

If that's the case, there might be more room for conscious intervention in our emotions than the hydraulic metaphor allows: euphoria, frustration, or chagrin are constructed categories that can be reimagined if we find that they don't serve us. When we speak or think about our feelings, we're not just describing what's going on inside us: in labeling the feeling, we bring it into being. Sometimes this is a social act. Think of a parent telling their child in the middle of a crying fit that they are angry, sad or "just tired": in a way they are instructing the child how to construct distinct emotions from the tangled mess inside. At other times we make an emotion real by speaking it aloud. The philosopher Bertrand Russell was struck by how his expression of love seemed to create the experience of it, rather than the other way around: "I did not know I loved you till I heard myself telling you so," he wrote in a letter to Lady Ottoline Morrell. "For one instance I thought, 'Good God, what have I said?' and then I knew it was the truth." Was the love lying dormant and undiscovered before, or was it conjured into existence by the magic words?

Inside out, or outside in?

In yet another intellectual tradition—typified by psychoanalysis—emotions might be a powerful force within us even if they remain unacknowledged. "Unexpressed emotions will never die," wrote Sigmund Freud. "They are buried alive and will come forth later in uglier ways." Over the course of the twentieth century—partly as a result of Freud's legacy—we have become increasingly comfortable with the idea that our emotions merit detailed attention and analysis: unearthing them can lead to important discoveries about the self.

There's a reason why the Pixar film was called *Inside Out*: it generally feels as though our emotions are personal, stemming from our individual experiences, and indeed sometimes so interior that we struggle to notice and identify them. But this isn't always the case; sometimes we can become swept up in emotion that is bigger than ourselves. Anthropologists often think of emotions like this: they are constructed not only psychologically (by our brains) but also by collective rituals and practices. This social form of emotion tends to emerge in group situations: the crowd's euphoria or misery at the final whistle of a football match, for example, or the mass outpouring of grief following the death of public figures such as Princess Diana or John F. Kennedy.

So emotions are everywhere: in the churning of your gut, the tingling of your skin, the intricate workings of your brain with all its conscious and semiconscious judgments—in the space between you and your companion as you negotiate the currents of feeling that pass between and around you. They are impulsive yet intellectual, biological and social, sometimes inconvenient but always indispensable.

Emotions are not one thing, but many. This book is a celebration and an exploration of that rich complexity.

Floriography
<u>FLORAL VOCABULARY</u>

Aster	Disturbed
Bellflower	Aggressive
Carnation (Red)	Defiant
Daffodil	Unaffectionate
Elderflower	Cold
Forget-Me-Not	Detached
Geranium	Callous
Hollyhock	Volatile
Iris	Violent
Lavender	Unemotional
Magnolia	Calculating
Nasturtium	Manipulative
Oxeye daisy	Predatory
Primrose	Impulsive
Poppy (Red)	Cruel
Rose (Pink)	Unrepentant
Snowdrop	Parasitic
Sunflower	Promiscuous
Tulip (White)	Irresponsible
Violet	Vengeful

Mark Dion, from *World in a Box*, 2015

1

ON THE INSIDE

EMOTIONAL HEAT MAPS

We often think about emotion in terms of temperature. When someone is quick to anger, they are "hot-headed." When they are empathetic and emotionally available, they are "warm-hearted." When an enthusiasm suddenly "cools" and the heat of your passion diminishes, you might say you have "cold feet."

The intense flushes of heat and cold that accompany shifting moods cannot be measured empirically: in scientific studies, emotion effects body heat negligibly, if at all. Yet the association between heat and feeling exists across periods and cultures.

The Ancient Greek philosopher Aristotle and the physician Galen both believed in a "vital heat," emanating from the soul and spreading throughout the body, transported by the blood. In the medicine of their time, the heart was not only figuratively but physiologically the seat of the passions. With each pulse it circulated the substance responsible for feelings and sensations that compose our moment-to-moment experience of ourselves.

Anger in particular is often identified with warmth. In European languages the metaphor often involves boiling fluids—what the philosopher Robert Solomon has called the "hydraulic metaphor." We are liable to bubble up, boil over, or burst out: like a steam engine in which pressure is constantly building, the gasket will blow if we don't "keep a lid on it."

In Chinese words and idioms, strong feelings such as anger are more often conceived as a hot air than as liquid or steam. This might have something to do with the notion of yin and yang, a fundamental aspect of classical Chinese thought. Of the two energies that determine the nature of all matter, yang is identified with heat and air; it is also identified with powerful passions (as opposed to cooler yin feelings like loneliness).

In 2013, a group of Finnish scientists set out to test commonalities among these associations between emotion and temperature. The researchers selected 701 participants from different linguistic backgrounds—including speakers of Finnish, Swedish, and Chinese—and showed them a selection of words, images, and videos designed to prime their emotional responses. For each emotion, the participants were asked to map onto a blank torso the parts of their body in which they experienced a sensation of cold or warmth.

The resulting body maps compose a striking atlas of human feeling. Happiness is manifested as a full-body glow. Anger and pride look curiously similar, with heat rising to the torso and head. Depression leaves the core untouched, but spreads a chill through the limbs and extremities. Sadness appears hot at the heart, but cold in the arms and legs.

These diagrams, a visualization of subjective bodily sensations rather than an empirical measure of temperature or energy flow—are intriguing and evocative. In the collision of physiology and metaphor, they capture something intangible and mysterious about the way the body makes emotions legible to the mind.

You don't need a lab to investigate your own topography of emotion. Trace an outline of a torso, tune into your body, and map what you feel in moments of relief, scorn, serenity, pity, or spite. How does it compare with the images opposite?

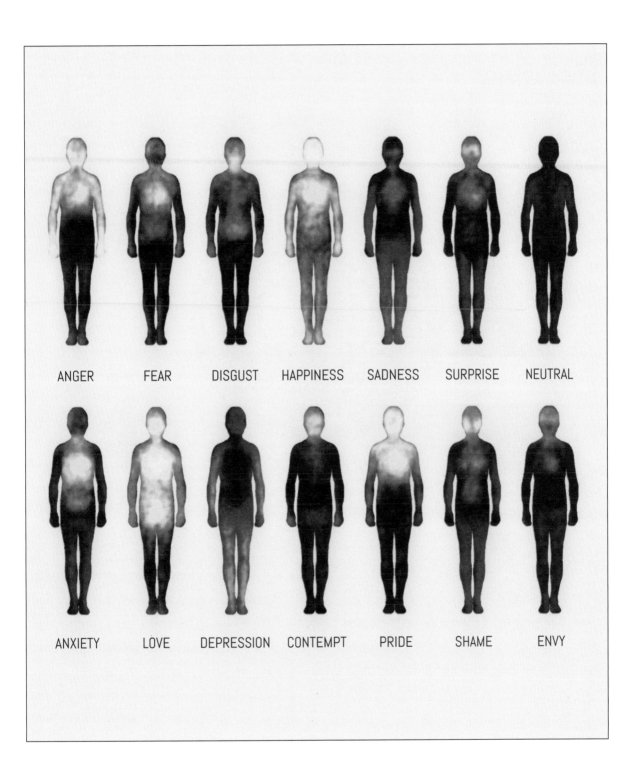

ANGER   FEAR   DISGUST   HAPPINESS   SADNESS   SURPRISE   NEUTRAL

ANXIETY   LOVE   DEPRESSION   CONTEMPT   PRIDE   SHAME   ENVY

EMOTIONS IN BODY AND MIND

NOGA ARIKHA

CHOLERIC

SANGUINE

MELANCHOLIC

PHLEGMATIC

A human life begins with feelings. A fetus already hears sounds from the mother's body and some from the outside world, and touches its own cheeks and hands. After birth, the baby feels light, noise, gravity, smells and tastes, and changes in temperature. Strange elements and other bodies touch the skin, which becomes a boundary with a new world made safe by the carers' holding and touch. There are bodily sensations of pleasure and pain, of hunger, thirst, hot, cold. As we grow, so we learn to differentiate progressively refined feelings.

Main image: The relation among the planets, the four temperaments, the four seasons, and the four elements, 1460. Courtesy National Library of the Netherlands. Smaller images from *Deutsche Kalendar*, 1498.

All living organisms must navigate their environment in order to survive, live, and reproduce. Emotions are responses to external stimuli—also called exteroception—and to internal bodily processes—called interoception. They arise as animals respond to objects that attract or repel them, to cues from other creatures, and to changes in the environment. But we are unique among animals in being able to think and talk about emotions, to name and share them: we are self-conscious creatures. We experience our emotions as feelings that we channel into our conscious, cognitive evaluations: of ourselves, of other people, of things, places, events, ideas, and opinions.

Because of our self-consciousness, humans have long tended to imagine a split between reason and emotions, and so between humans and the rest of nature. Our smarts, and indeed our capacity to rationalize emotions, have ensured that we dominate the globe. But awareness of the increasingly invasive effects of human productivity on all of life on Earth is one factor that has led to the resurgence of another, equally ancient view: that humans are on a continuum with the whole of nature and that emotions are on a continuum with "higher" faculties. For 2,500 years, there prevailed the notion that our emotional states, our character, and our states of health and illness were conditioned by so-called humors. These were substances that the ancient Greeks had first imagined flowed through the body. All of us harbored all humors in differing proportions. Connected to this humoral theory was the notion, derived mainly from Aristotle, that mental functions were distributed throughout the body: the rational soul unique to humans was located in the brain; the heart was the seat of the sensitive soul, which processed emotions all animals experienced; and the liver housed the appetitive soul, which processed nutrition and reproduction and was common to all living organisms. These organs were anatomically and humorally connected to one another; hence, reason and emotion were constantly interacting. Key to this fundamentally holistic view was the notion that a state of health is one in which our humors are in a state of balance. Ill health was believed to occur when this balance is disrupted, most notably when there is an excess of black bile: melancholy is "black bile" in Greek, *melaina chole*—this was thought to cause all manner of delusional, manic, or generally miserable states, as catalogued by Robert Burton in his *Anatomy of Melancholy*, first published in 1621.

Modern medicine discarded humors as the imaginary or at most the figurative constructs they indeed were. Yet in dissolving the psychosomatic model of the organism something was lost. Medicine became increasingly mechanistic, a psychiatry focused on neurotransmitters—as if the brain could exist without the body. For a while scientists, philosophers, and social scientists tended to ignore emotions, which they considered too subjective to study and irrelevant to the "higher" cognitive faculties so specific to humans.

But over the past three decades, the scientific study of emotions, including affective neuroscience, has rendered possible the investigation of emotions both as features of a mind that cannot exist without the body and as an integral and essential feature of subjective and social experience. Within the social sciences, in turn, researchers have been recognizing that the thinking, rational mind is connected to our affect, and that affective processes are embodied.

And so, the old, commonsensical idea of humoral balance is echoed in the notion of homeostasis that is central to the understanding of emotions: first coined in the early twentieth century by physiologist Walter Cannon, homeostasis is the constant adjustment of the body's physiology in response to unceasing changes in the environment. Single cells engage in it, and so do complex organisms—ourselves included. The visceral signals that translate into interoception and are the basis for emotions correspond to these homeostatic processes. The new research on interoception centers on our embodied, animal selves, whose nervous systems process emotions as well as thoughts. It offers the possibility of viewing the emotions of our physical organism, such as the feelings we call happiness, sadness, fear, and anger, on a continuum with the more elaborate social emotions, such as jealousy, guilt, trust, or compassion, that are variously the glue of all human societies. Our biological bodies become social and political bodies, via affective states that give rise to emotionally rich cultures of words, arts, and representations.

We have finally accepted the notion that we are emoting, physical beings and that we are biologically cultural. But we are still exploring the consequences of this approach for the understanding of our place in nature and of ourselves and each other as individuals, as groups, and as cultures.

Friedrich Kunath, *Actually, I Don't*, 2012

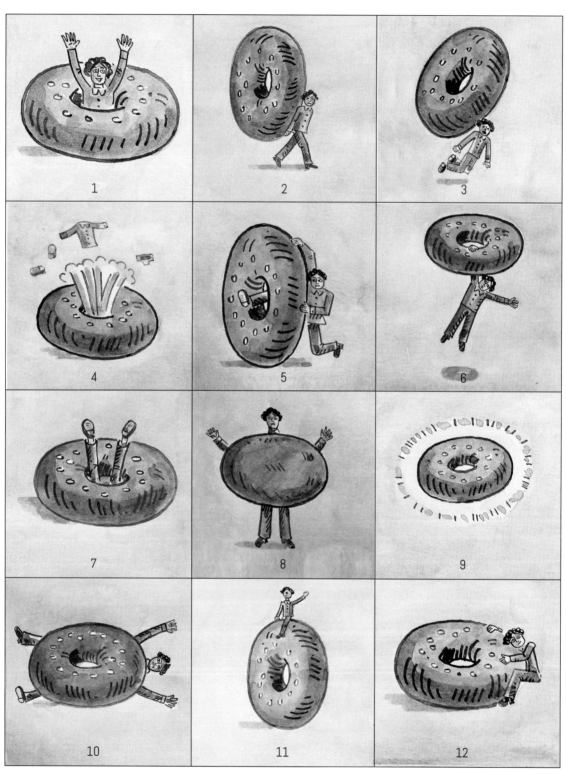

Illustration by Adam Dant

HOW DO YOU FEEL?

What emotion you feel at any given moment is a hard enough question to answer. But how you relate to your emotions is another question altogether. Even though we tend to think of emotions as an intimate part of our inner selves, we often talk about them in ways that imply that they are something separate from ourselves. Everyday language is infused with such metaphors—each one suggesting a different role that emotions might play in our psychology.

Pick the cartoon that best illustrates the way you tend to experience your feelings and turn over the page to find out what that might say about your relationship with emotions.

1. Wallowing in it

We generally think of emotions as being something that happens within us, as though we are the containers and they are the contents. But sometimes the way we describe our feelings suggests exactly the opposite. We wallow in misery, bask in pride, luxuriate in pleasure or grief. That's what emotions are to you: an ambient sensation to relax into and appreciate—even if on the surface they might seem negative. Wallowing in an emotion gets a bad rap, since it implies a certain amount of self-involvement. But you're not suppressing or rejecting it, at least.

2. Carrying it as a burden

You experience emotions as a great load that you must dutifully carry with you despite its oppressive weight. Guilt is one emotion that is frequently talked about as a burden, but it could also be sorrow or disappointment—or even an ostensibly positive emotion, such as hope. You are the servant of your feelings—and they are a hard master. If you can't find a way to let them go, at least try to share the load.

3. Being struck by it

Feelings descend on you suddenly and violently, like a bolt of lightning, a heavenly chorus, or an anvil from the clear blue sky. We sometimes say that we are struck by an emotion or that we experience it like a punch to the gut. The feelings themselves might not always be bad, but they are abrupt and unexpected. Perhaps your emotions are just unpredictable. But it may well be that you are in the habit of ignoring or denying them until they become too powerful to overlook.

4. Full of it / overflowing with it

You are a vessel for emotions that you struggle to contain. Perhaps you are filled with gratitude or overflowing with love. Or perhaps you are brimming with indignation or rage. In any case, your scarcely suppressed feelings constantly threaten to spill over into the world. The challenge is to find a way of letting them out without harming yourself or anybody else.

5. Wrestling / struggling with it

You are locked in a furious struggle with feelings you do not want to accept. Perhaps you are wrestling your fear or struggling to contain your anger. Perhaps you are battling an ill-fated infatuation. "You can't fight the feeling," they say—but that hasn't stopped you from trying.

6. Being carried away by it

It seems that you have willingly given over control to your emotions and are letting them take you on whatever journey they have planned.

7. Immersed in it / falling into it

Sometimes emotions are so overpowering that they seem to engulf us completely: we fall in love or are swallowed up with hate or shame. You might not have sought these passions, but now they are all around you.

8. Being consumed by it

You feel yourself to be consumed by your emotions, eaten up by passions more powerful than your will. Often these are the passions of Shakespearean tragedy: pride, rage, jealousy, ambition. Perhaps you should reconsider your relationship with those passions.

9. Haunted by it

Your emotions are a ghostly presence lingering tantalizingly somewhere in your conscious or unconscious mind. The most common version of this emotional condition occurs when your dominant feelings are attached to events that are in the distant past: you may be haunted by regret or remorse. Alternatively, it may be that your feelings are hard to grasp or define: you are haunted by uncertainty. Like all self-respecting ghosts, these emotions will persist until they find resolution.

10. Being crushed by it

You experience your emotions as both hostile and overpowering: you are helpless beneath their cruel weight. We talk about being crushed by feelings like shame, grief, or despair. Things are bad right now—but it's possible to reconceive your feelings as something less antagonistic and irresistible.

11. Riding high on it

You are riding high on a feeling—happiness, confidence, requited love. In this rare and blessed state, emotion is like a breeze or a cloud that is effortlessly buoying you up: all you need to do is waft on its easy winds. A cautious person might warn of the dangers of crashing back down to earth—but why waste time thinking about worst-case scenarios when your feelings are treating you so right?

12. Nursing it

Some people fight their feelings or quail before their irresistible might. Not you. Instead, you are cultivating an emotional state, attentively nurturing a feeling that some part of you wants or needs. Sometimes this can be a perverse impulse—for instance, when we nurse a sense of grievance. But it can also be a kind of self-care—for instance, you might foster your compassion or empathy. Just make sure that the feeling you're feeding won't grow into something terrifying and cruel.

ARCS OF TRIUMPH (AND DISASTER)

Kurt Vonnegut was one of the twentieth century's most beloved American writers. But in Vonnegut's own estimation, his "prettiest contribution to the culture" came not in the form of a novel or play but in a brief lecture delivered in 1995. In this lecture he sketched out an idea that he believed offered the key to understanding the basic structure of all narratives in human culture. Vonnegut's arcs of storytelling offer a simple, graphic method for mapping every story, from the New Testament to *When Harry Met Sally*.

On the y-axis he plotted the emotional well-being conveyed by the story and experienced by the main character (their happiness, their prosperity, their exposure to peril). The x-axis was the progression of the story over time. Vonnegut's theory was that the vast majority of story arcs—be they ancient myths, gothic novels, Disney films, epic poems, or folk ballads—followed one of a few basic trajectories. Here they are:

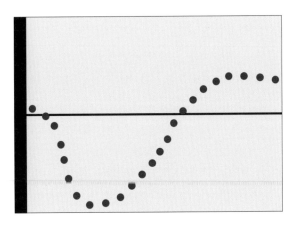

1) Man in a hole: The protagonist's life is going smoothly enough, until there is a sudden catastrophe. Perhaps they don't literally fall in a hole, but the disaster they encounter transforms their life so that all of their attention becomes directed toward resolving the problem. They spend the rest of the story recovering their previous equilibrium, but when they finally do, they generally find that their life is even better than it had been to begin with.

Examples: *The Lord of the Rings, 101 Dalmatians, Desperately Seeking Susan*

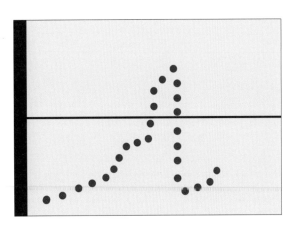

2) Rags to riches: Our hero begins the story at rock bottom, miserable, hopeless, and alone. Then an opportunity presents itself and their life gradually improves. Step by step, they begin to work themselves up from nothing...but just as total fulfillment is in sight, something happens that risks losing it all. Perhaps their carriage turns into a pumpkin; perhaps they eat the forbidden fruit of a mysterious tree. But just when all hope seems lost, one last miracle (whether it's in the form of a messiah or a glass slipper) secures their everlasting bliss.

Examples: *Cinderella, Annie, David Copperfield*

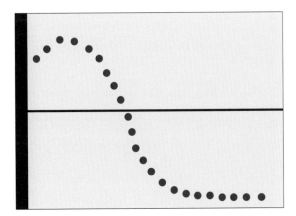

3) Riches to rags/Oedipus: Like number two, but in reverse: a person has everything they could want, but gradually loses it all. Perhaps their gains were ill-gotten and their fall from grace was warranted; perhaps they were ungrateful with their lot and foolishly shot for the moon when they should have stuck with the good things they had; perhaps all their good fortune was an illusion to begin with, gradually evaporating in contact with reality.

Examples: *Citizen Kane, Madame Bovary, Frankenstein*

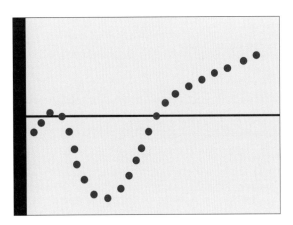

4) Boy meets girl: The protagonist has a humdrum life—nothing too miserable but lacking something to give it meaning. Suddenly their existence is illuminated by the possibility of previously unimaginable joy. Often that comes in the shape of true love, but it could be anything: great riches, a true home, a political cause. But just as a better existence begins to materialize, it is snatched away. The rest of the narrative is a quest to recover it.

Examples: *Jane Eyre, Titanic, Notting Hill*

But what about those stories that don't fit any of these arcs? In which the twists and the turns of the plot are myriad and difficult to trace? Or in which many protagonists with conflicting fortunes compete for our sympathy and attention? Or there is no plot at all, or it's impossible to know what's good or bad? Vonnegut also recognized the existence of such stories, and in his view these were the greatest stories of all: they recognized that human experience was too messy and multifaceted to be reduced to a two-dimensional arc. His chosen example of this complex story arc was *Hamlet*: it's never easy to tell whether the king's fortunes are improving or deteriorating, or what would constitute a happy ending.

Perhaps the emotional journey of a real person's life is too complex to map neatly. But Vonnegut (admittedly with tongue in cheek) described his methods as a scientific approach to literary criticism, and in this empirical spirit, there is only one objective way to test his conclusions.

On the facing page are two charts designed to help you and your family record your own emotional narrative arcs. Scan it or photocopy it and, over the course of a day, use it to plot the trajectory of your fortunes and your sense of well-being. Each family member should use a different colored pencil: at the end of the day much may be revealed.

	MONDAY		TUESDAY		WEDNESDAY		THURSDAY		FRIDAY		SATURDAY		SUNDAY	
	AM	PM	AM	PM	AM	PM	AM	PM	AM	PM	AM	PM	AM	PM
EUPHORIC														
JOYFUL														
CHEERY														
SERENE														
FINE														
BLANK														
GLOOMY														
MOROSE														
MISERABLE														
DESOLATE														

	JAN	FEB	MAR	APR	MAY	JUN	JUL	AUG	SEPT	OCT	NOV	DEC
EUPHORIC												
JOYFUL												
CHEERY												
SERENE												
FINE												
BLANK												
GLOOMY												
MOROSE												
MISERABLE												
DESOLATE												

James McNeill Whistler, *Weary*, 1863

2

EXPRESSION

FACES OF FEELING

At this moment, in a university laboratory or the engine room of a tech start-up, a computer is learning to read your face. The aim is not merely to recognize your identity but to gauge the inner workings of your mind. Every moment, the theory goes, the small dramas of your moment-to-moment emotional experience are playing out in the micro-expressions of your face. A slight narrowing of the eyes for a split second might signal a twinge of suspicion; a barely perceptible twitch of your lower lip might communicate amusement or irritation. The software will pick up on feelings that you're not even aware of, and the information it gathers will be used to make decisions that could affect the course of your life. Perhaps it will determine which advertisements you are shown on social media, whether you get a job, or whether you are convicted of a crime.

That's the theory, anyway—there are plenty of skeptics. Are our innermost feelings really so legible? Can we really create a universal typology of emotions, with a distinctive set of facial contortions to match each one?

Twenty-first-century computers are far from the first to attempt to crack this code. The idea that we could create a definitive dictionary for translating facial expressions directly into emotional experiences has fascinated psychologists and artists for centuries. The resulting profusion of girning, grinning, grimacing faces offers a lesson in how elusive the universal language of emotion really is.

1: CHARLES LE BRUN

Charles Le Brun was a seventeenth-century painter who was convinced that he had found the key to the fundamental nature of feelings. The passions, he believed were "movements of the soul" that reverberated throughout the body in the form of psychic energy. The role of facial expressions was to channel this soul energy in response to objects in the world.

A person in the grip of admiration or wonder was pouring their spirit out toward the world; that is why their eyes would grow wide and their mouth and brow form a circle, redirecting the energy of the soul from within to stream toward whatever the person is admiring. "If the heart is dejected," on the other hand, "all parts of the face will be cast down."

Le Brun gathered these insights from an analysis of portraiture, which he understood as the science of human character. He believed that great painters were endowed with a divinely inspired comprehension of the human form and an ability to portray each emotion as an ideal type: Michelangelo's painting of a pensive angel expressed pensiveness more powerfully than any real person ever could. But would you recognize these emotions? Or does this *désespoir* seem to the modern eye like another emotion altogether?

A face with hair on end, expressing a state of despair. Engraving by W. Hebert, c. 1770, after Charles Le Brun
Four faces expressing the human passions. Engraving by I. O. Barlow, 19th century, after Charles Le Brun

Wonder / fear / astonishment. From *Essays on the Anatomy of Expression in Painting*, 1806. Engraving by Sir Charles Bell

External signs of the passions. Engraving by J. Pass, early 19th century, after Charles Le Brun

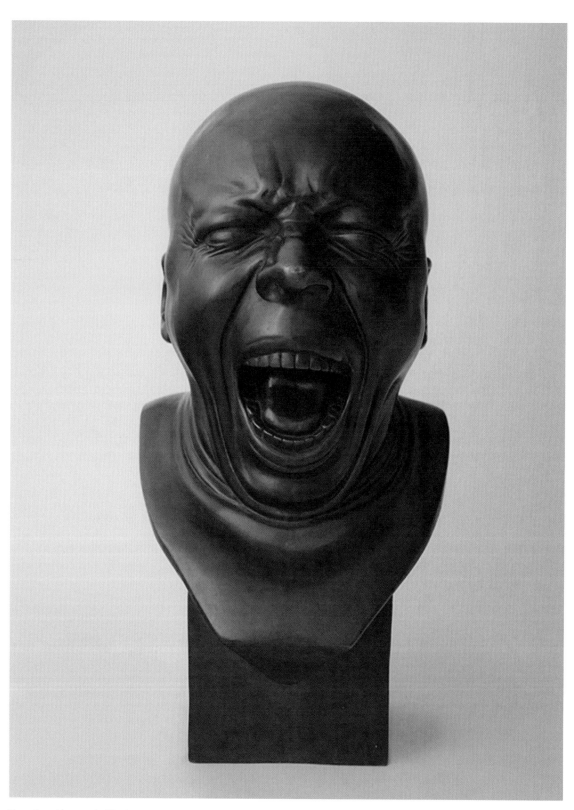

Franz Xaver Messerschmidt, character head no. 5, 18th century

2: FRANZ XAVER MESSERSCHMIDT

When Franz Xaver Messerschmidt died in 1783, he left behind very few material possessions. Poor, isolated, and mentally ill, he had been cast out of the Viennese artistic society to which he had belonged. He lived his final years in a small mountain hut, furnished with barely anything besides a bed. His only possessions were fifty-six startling and utterly unique sculptures: self-portraits modeled on his head, each contorted into a different arrangement of sinew and flesh—each idiosyncratic, intricate, and bizarre.

Messerschmidt believed that the human face could arrange itself into exactly sixty-four different grimaces, each responding to its own particular sensibility or mood. Plagued by tormenting thoughts and feelings, he believed that he could exorcise his demons by casting their physiological manifestations in metal and stone. A malicious ghost that Messerschmidt labeled the "spirit of proportions" visited him during the night and "pinched" him. The sculptures were the artist's attempts to pinch the demon back.

It's easy to see these sculptures as symptoms of madness or depression—and surely that's at least partly what they are. But they are also anatomically precise and organized with a rigour that rivals more systematic theorists like Charles Darwin and Charles Le Brun.

Franz Xaver Messerschmidt, character head no. 6, 18th century

Franz Xaver Messerschmidt, character head no. 11, 18th century

3: CHARLES DARWIN / DUCHENNE DE BOULOGNE

While writing *The Descent of Man*, the British naturalist Charles Darwin became fascinated with the origin and meaning of expressions—so much so that it became the subject of his following book. For years, Darwin intently analyzed the twitches of the faces of his children, his friends, and passing strangers. He scrutinized the exact muscles that were engaged in his children's lips as they quivered before they cried. He demanded accounts from friends with babies, whom he believed to show emotions in their purest possible forms. He analyzed photographs of actors who were reputed to be capable of replicating "authentic" expressions with uncanny perfection. He even drew on macabre research by the French physician Duchenne de Boulogne, who had fitted convicted criminals with electrodes and delivered small shocks to their facial muscles in an attempt to replicate natural human expressions.

Darwin was determined to prove that, contrary to earlier theories (including Le Brun's), human expressions were neither divinely inspired reflections of the soul nor unique to humans. Curiously, he didn't believe that the purpose of expressions was to communicate feelings. Instead, he thought that they were side effects of shifts in the body that had once had a practical purpose. If you are angry, you lift your lip to show your teeth. Darwin understood this as a remnant of an impulse to bite somebody.

Darwin's theories are still controversial today. Some psychologists resist the idea that expressions can be codified in this way or that facial expressions have such a starkly practical cause. On the other hand, these theories have been influential in the development of the microexpression software that could soon be interpreting every fleeting furrow of your brow...

 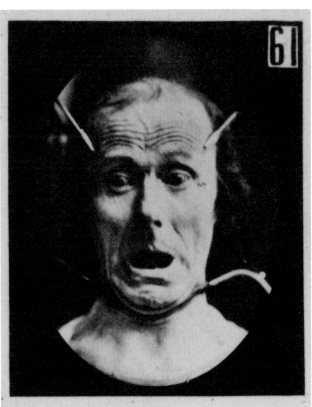

"Frowning" and "Fear" from Duchenne de Boulogne, *Mécanisme de la Physionomie Humaine*, 1862

Smiling

Surprise

Hopelessness / Impotence

Moderate laughter / Joy

Devotion

Surprise / Astonishment

LEFT: From Charles Darwin, *The Expression of the Emotions in Man and Animals*   ABOVE: Pride

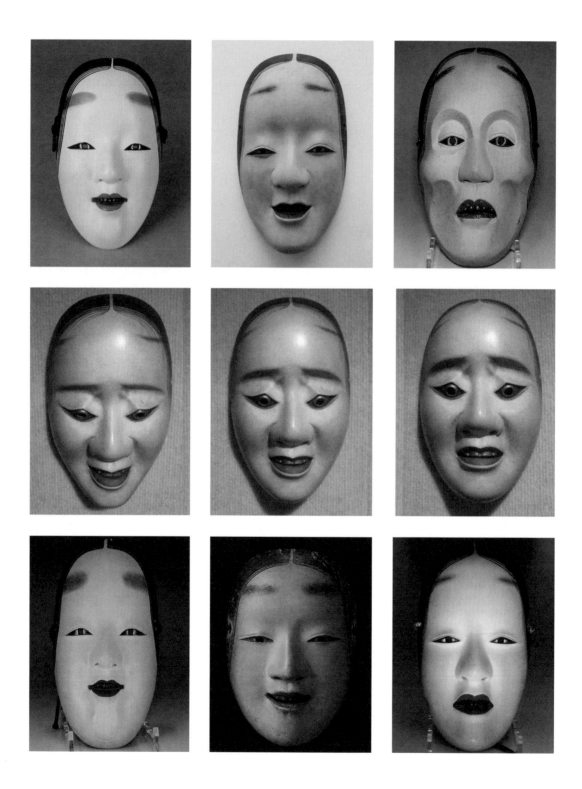

NOH MASKS

Tilted downward, the mask looks like an enigmatic smile. Tilt it upward, and the smile becomes a menacing frown. Tricks of light and perspective enable the wearer to become a sort of emotional chameleon, skillfully choreographing their movements to convey a flux of symbolic passions.

Noh masks are designed to make the invisible visible by portraying the conflict of spiritual forces as a psychological drama, playing out on the human face. The expression on each mask is fixed and conveys the archetype it represents, while changes in feeling are represented by the actor's arms. However, the masks are also constructed in such a way that the emotion appears to change as shadows play across it: a mask that generally suggests happiness might look angry as the actor shifts skillfully under the dramatic light.

In other words, the mask expresses two layers of emotional state: the unshifting grooves and contours of a character type, which are carved into the wood itself, and the ephemeral feelings that become evident in the mask's interaction with its environment. This reflects an insight about the nature of emotions themselves: in part they are a product of our inaccessible, internal selves and in part a product of the outside world and its provocations.

Noh masks have been taken to exemplify another core tenet of traditional Japanese psychology and metaphysics: the idea that the highest goal in life and art is to see and understand the essence of things and to live according to your most authentic nature. Acting in the purest sense can't be simply imitative. Instead, it must be a transformative act in which the actors align themselves with something universal in the emotions they express. They do this by stepping outside of themselves and seeing themselves as though through the eyes of the audience. For this purpose there is a mirror to the side of the stage; this also is part of the purpose of the mask. "The functions of mirror and mask merge as a spirit is incarnated and the self is transformed by the magic of strengthened autosuggestion," as Kunio Komparu, an expert on Noh masks, has put it.

Although Noh theater is a living art form in Japan, it has declined in recent decades. The masks have found a new and unexpected life as objects in psychological studies. The fact that these solid, unpliable objects can be used to suggest various emotional states has fascinated neuroscientists searching for indications of sadness in brain chemistry. One study uses Noh masks to search for symptoms of mental disorders that prevent people from recognizing subtle indications of an emotion. Another uses the mask to locate the neural signs of what, in a strikingly poetic phrase, the scientists term "delicate sadness."

THE LANDSCAPE TEST

Which landscape do you feel matches your state of mind today?

The paintings on the following pages reflect their creators' mood. Look through them and try to enter their imaginative or emotional worlds. Then pick which painting you most identify with and turn to pages 72–73 find out what your choice may mean.

In *Modern Painters*, vol. 3, 1856, John Ruskin proposed the term *pathetic fallacy*—the idea that depictions of the natural world can express the artist's emotional state. He explained his concept using an example from Charles Kingsley's novel *Alton Locke:* "They rowed her in across the rolling foam—The cruel, crawling foam."

The foam is not cruel, neither does it crawl. The state of mind which attributes to it these characters of a living creature is one in which the reason is unhinged by grief. All violent feelings have the same effect. They produce in us a falseness in all our impressions of external things, which I would generally characterize as the "pathetic fallacy."...

The temperament which admits the pathetic fallacy, is, as I said above, that of a mind and body in some sort too weak to deal fully with what is before them or upon them; borne away, or over-clouded, or over-dazzled by emotion; and it is a more or less noble state, according to the force of the emotion which has induced it. For it is no credit to a man that he is not morbid or inaccurate in his perceptions, when he has no strength of feeling to warp them; and it is in general a sign of higher capacity and stand in the ranks of being, that the emotions should be strong enough to vanquish, partly, the intellect, and make it believe what they choose...

My reason for asking the reader to give so much of his time to the examination of the pathetic fallacy was, that, whether in literature or in art, he will find it eminently characteristic of the modern mind; and in the landscape, whether of literature or art, he will also find the modern painter endeavoring to express something which he, as a living creature, imagines in the lifeless object.

1

2

4

7

1) Albert Pinkham Ryder, *Moonlit Cove*, early to mid-1880s

A round moon glows over a still, hazy sea. But rather than illuminating the cove, it throws it into shadow: the shape of a boat standing at rest in the gloom is so faint that you may not even have noticed it at first glance. This painting suggests an outwardly calm mental state—perhaps even a sort of reverie—that gives little hint of the romantic stirrings that lurk beneath the surface, of emotions ominous or sublime.

2) Eric Ravilious, *The Causeway, Wiltshire Downs*, 1937

A harmonious, bucolic scene of undulating pastures suggests a cheery and contented disposition. Nature and the human world are at ease; the colors are lively yet gentle; picturesque clouds adorn a blue sky. The work apparently reflects the disposition of its creator: "I never saw him depressed," a close friend said of Ravilious. "Even when he fell in love—and that was frequently—he was never submerged by disappointment. Cheerfulness kept creeping in."

3) Isaac Levitan, *The Vladimirka Road*, 1892

The flat monotony of this dirt road speaks of something worse than mere boredom. The looming sky, the shadowy figure in the middle distance, the oddly gray tones—a sense of latent anxiety and menace pervades the scene. This is not surprising once you know the hidden message behind this painting. The Vladimir Highway was the road that carried convicts to the infamous Siberian prison colonies, and this painting was a coded attack on the imperial regime responsible for such atrocities. The path leads only to misery and despair.

4) Paul Gauguin, *La Vague*, 1888

The two people in the corner of the painting are presumably bathing for pleasure, and the seascape they inhabit is indeed vivid and dynamic. But it's far from being a safe space. They are at the mercy of a surging, roiling sea, peppered with forbidding black rocks, which seems to claw at them even as they play. The mood is one of exhilaration, but also of danger and a vertiginous lack of control.

5) Vincent van Gogh, *Starry Night*, 1889

A richly vivid night sky churns and swirls above a village in the valley, its blues and yellows warmly suffusing the scene. This dreamlike image is one of the most famous landscapes ever painted. Yet critics have never been able to agree whether it is a vision of fantasia or the apocalypse. Van Gogh painted it from an asylum while recovering from a mental health crisis in which he amputated his own ear. But the period of his convalescence, in a beautiful hilly region of Provence, was one of the more peaceful of his troubled life. Whether this picture expresses horror or elation, it clearly tells of an intensely feeling mind.

6) Vincent van Gogh, *Landscape with Carriage and Trains*, 1890

Rustic landscapes are usually sedate, but this one feels full of movement and noise: the vehicles in the title suggest a more frenetic world beyond the farmland that is immediately visible, and even the fields themselves seem agitated. "Lately I've been working a lot and quickly," van Gogh wrote in a letter at the time he painted this. "By doing so I'm trying to express the desperately swift passage of things in modern life." A restless scenery indicates a restless mind.

7) Kazimir Malevich, *Spring*, 1920s

Calm, bright, and exquisite, this vision of a crisp spring day immediately suggests happiness and hope. But there is also a hint of fragility and impermanence: the frail trees dissolving into the landscape like ghosts. Perhaps the joy this is describing is a half-remembered feeling, or one that comes with the knowledge of its own passing— something like the Japanese phrase *mono no aware*, which describes an awareness of great beauty combined with the sorrowful knowledge that it will pass.

ANIMAL PASSIONS

For a long time, scientists considered the idea that animals have feelings in any way comparable to those of humans to be sentimental and suspiciously anthropomorphic. The rationalist dismissal of animal emotions began in the seventeenth century with René Descartes, who denied that animals have souls or subjective lives, and was buttressed by twentieth-century experimenters who were keen to justify the vivisection that provided fuel for their research.

Recently, however, the idea that animals have a rich inner life (which most ordinary pet owners would never have doubted) has started to reenter the scientific mainstream. But animals don't always exhibit their feelings in ways that are easily legible to us. Opposite is a selection of animals expressing various feelings. Can you guess which is which? Answers are on the next page.

pleasure/contentment	self-consciousness
distress	excitement (possibly sexual)

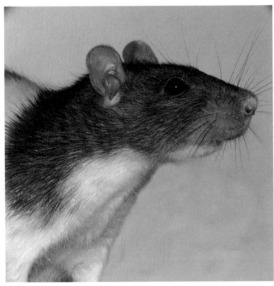

Rat: pleasure / contentment

Few if any animals have been as closely observed by scientists as the humble rat. But it was only recently that researchers first noticed a subtle way in which their favorite minions were exhibiting signs of pleasure: when they are enjoying a sensation or a snack or just generally feeling comfortable, rats' ears go bright pink.

Chameleon: excited

When we describe someone as a chameleon, we generally mean they have a mercurial ability to adapt and blend in. But camouflage isn't the only reason for chameleons' kaleidoscopic skins: the lattice of crystals on their scales shifts to display different colors depending on their emotional state. When lizards are aroused, they show bright colors like red, yellow, and orange; when they are scared and submissive, they become dull and dark.

Chimp: distress

Apes and monkeys have a range of facial expressions, some of which correspond quite closely with those of humans. But they can still be inscrutable: this chimp might appear puzzled, focused, or mischievous, but it is actually exhibiting discomfort or distress.

Macaw: self-conscious

This one's a bit of a guess; nobody really knows why certain species of parrot blush, but blush they do. What suggests that their flushed cheeks might have a similar meaning to those of humans is that they seem to exhibit the behavior only when they are aware that they are being watched. Parrots are increasingly thought to be some of the smartest nonhuman animals—might they have reached the same level of uncomfortable self-awareness as an awkward teenager?

WHAT MAKES YOU MAD?

This list is based on an informal diagnostic device whose purpose is to help people gauge the extent to which they get annoyed with certain often-encountered situations or types of behavior. Simply count how many items on the list you find unbearably annoying. A very low score (under 5) indicates that you tend to be patient with others' foibles and unaffected by trivial irritations. It probably means that you also have low levels of stress. A very high score (over 12) suggests irascibility. You are too easily stressed, so try to take things a bit easier! If your score is medium, then, as for almost anybody, there are certain things you can't help getting annoyed by. Don't worry! Just don't let too many things get to you: life is too short to spend it in a permanent frenzy of irritation. If absolutely nothing in the list annoys you, then you are either deeply eccentric or a saint.

Parents discussing their children's virtues and achievements

Dentists who ask you questions when it's impossible to answer

A person who asks for, and then instantly ignores, your advice

Passengers on a busy train who claim a whole seat for their baggage

Shop assistants who will not leave you alone

Yoga teachers who single you out for attention

Ailment one-upmanship

Demonstrative sighing

Brands or public service announcements attempting to be kooky and chirpy

Anecdotes related to excessive alcohol or drug consumption

Couples staging theatrical disagreements in company

Humble-bragging

Being passed (while driving/swimming/cycling) by someone who then immediately slows down

People who pick at the best parts of a dish and leave you the rest

A weak handshake

Highly successful people talking about how inefficient they are

Meeting a friend who looks at their phone every time they get an alert

Things that won't fit back in the box from which they have just been removed

Being told to calm down

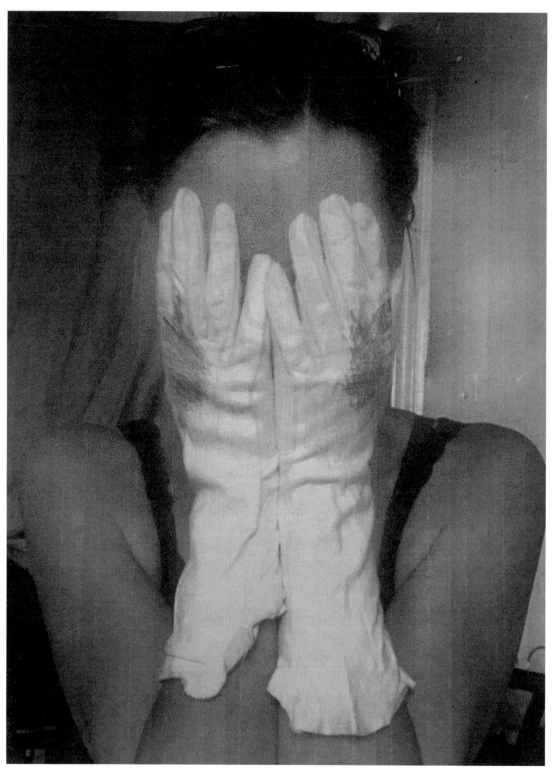

Self Portrait in Kid Gloves, pastel on photocopy paper, 2018

BLUSHING
CHARLES BOYLE / IMAGES BY NATALIA ZAGÓRSKA-THOMAS

A blush is warm. A blush can feel as if it's about to gobble me up. A blush is as involuntary as laughter or tears or a scream or a grimace or a yawn or fainting, and a blush speaks true, even if its truth is a puzzle—something about the body and the social context in which that body finds itself having to live and how the mind struggles to cope with all the mixed messages.

A blush is not itself an emotion but a bringing to the surface—the cheek of it!—of emotions that are imprecise and often contradictory.

A blush is more of a question than an answer. A bewilderment. A panic button.

A blush is a quick-motion bruise. A blush is a passing wound, subcutaneous, the blood seeking release but the skin holding tight. The heart races.

Blushing is a social mechanism whose purpose is obscure and it's probably best that way, because awkwardness and not-knowing are what make it, according to Charles Darwin, "the most human of all expressions."

Darwin in *The Expression of Emotions in Man and Animals* (1872) proposed that blushing is induced by "shyness, shame, and modesty." All of these are socially conditioned. He observed that "women blush more than men" because the narrative of shame—who has to feel it, who doesn't—is written by men. And that "the young blush much more frequently than the old" because during adolescence comfort blankets and fairy tales are still boiling in the pot together with all the new ingredients—discovery of the world and rational enquiry—and the body is going a bit wild and the gas is on high. Of course the cheeks get hot.

The poems of John Keats, the critic Christopher Ricks observes, "are full of blushes"—as they are too of quiverings, oozings, swellings, and seepings, all of which are a kind of trespassing. The word *embarrassment* didn't acquire its modern meaning until the late eighteenth century, Ricks notes, and in the following century "blushing and embarrassment came to be thought of as crucial to a great many social and moral matters." The novel in its most familiar guise—a tool for investigating how individuals react to the pressures of their environment, for playing off desires and aspirations against social codes—got into its stride during the same period, and a blush was also playing merry hell on maps of the world over a quarter of the world's land surface, the color of the British Empire. In "Maud" (1855) by Alfred Lord Tennyson, England's poet laureate, male sexual conquest is celebrated as an ever-expanding imperial blush: "When the happy Yes / Falters from her lips, / Pass and blush the news / O'er the blowing ships. / Over blowing seas…"

In the nineteenth century marriage market, a woman's blush signified a virtuous reputation; that it had an erotic allure, suggesting sexual feeling under restraint, was a bonus. By 1904 the London tattooist George Burchett was inflicting "permanent delicate, pink blushes on ladies' cheeks." "A chaste and charming blush," *Tatler* reported. The *Daily Mail:* "The rosy cheeks that rival Nature at her best."

Jabot, mixed media with kid glove, 2014

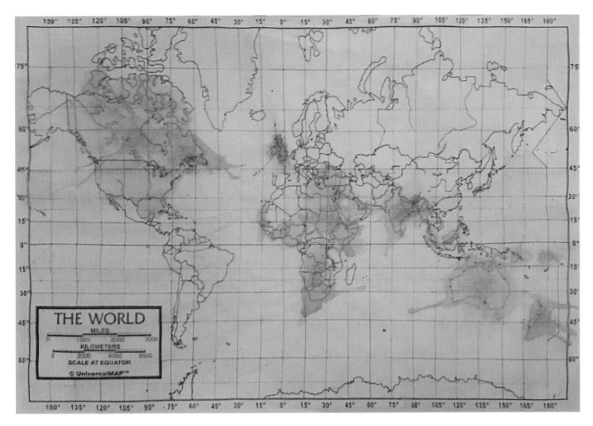

The World, gouache on photocopy paper, 2018

Since the late nineteenth century, the blush has been coarsened: cosmeticized, marginalized, monetized…Pasted like emoji into the plots of traditional romance fiction, blushes ("bashful," "virginal," "maidenly") add a little light sexual frisson.

As taboos crumble and as privacy is surrendered to surveillance cameras and to corporations that track online clicks—and this data is packaged and sold on, and on again—is there anything left to feel shy or shameful about? Is the blush as passé as the curtsey or the bow? Do we even care?

The body still cares. Blushing is essentially a social activity—the extreme self-consciousness associated with blushing depends entirely on awareness of others—and our freedom from outdated social and sexual prohibitions does not put an end to the continual negotiation between our private and our public selves.

A chink, a gap, a little slippage between me and the other me, the one I'm performing—where the blush gets in…

As a badge of discomfort and disarray and confusion, the blush is an admission that the world is a mystery. We are less in control than we'd like to believe we are. We don't know other people—know them well, know them fully—and we don't know ourselves. We don't even know, most of us, how our computers and smartphones and satnavs work: as at a societal level technological know-how increases, so at an individual level does ignorance. We know precious little about love and about history and about what it is to be born and to die, and the little that we do know we are very bad at passing on to others, and whatever embarrassment prompts our blushes is essentially embarrassment at our not-knowing, along with a vague feeling that for reasons we can never properly spell out we are somehow *in the wrong.*

A blush is a flag of inconvenience, a busted flush, a gulp, a glitch, a stammer, a flutter, a flinch. In embarrassment, head down and hands to cheeks, shielding, protective—a movement as involuntary as the blush itself.

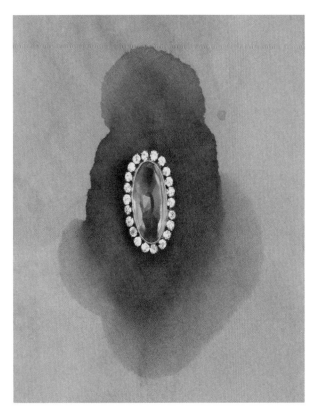

National University, Kiev, Ukraine, iPhone photograph, 2016   *Stain, Camden Town, London*, iPhone photograph, 2016

THE EYES HAVE IT

The eyes are the window to the soul, or so they say. What is going on behind the irises of each of these characters from a classic film?

1

a) Lust
b) Envy
c) Malice

2

a) Fear
b) Reverence
c) Rage

3

a) Bafflement
b) Suspiciousness
c) Irritation

4

a) Impotent hatred
b) Thwarted love
c) Ennui

5

a) Pity
b) Dread and despair
c) Bitter mirth

6

a) Fury
b) Terror
c) Greed

7

a) Joyful abandon
b) Empathy
c) Regret

8

a) Love
b) Hate
c) Love and hate

1c

This is Nurse Ratched from *One Flew Over the Cuckoo's Nest*. Jack Nicholson's Randy McMurphie, a patient, has just raised an objection to Ratched's tyranny over the psychiatric ward, and she is plotting the next move in their fatal power struggle. Ratched is in many ways the archetype of an evil bureaucrat, but her malevolence is tempered by an ostensibly gentle manner. It's a portrayal of feminine tyranny that has since been criticized as a misogynist paranoid fantasy: a woman in a position of authority who behaves like a dark distortion of the mother figure.

2c

"I'm mad as hell and I'm not gonna take it anymore!" This scene from *Network* is one of the most famous rants in cinema history: a rogue news presenter goes off script and calls on his viewers to tune into their rage, sparked by his daily litany of miseries and catastrophes. "I don't know what to do about the depression and the inflation and the Russians and the crime in the street," he is saying. "All I know is that first you've got to get mad." Made in 1976, *Network* has since come to seem prophetic amid the rise of political anger and anxiety and amid collapsing boundaries between media and politics.

3b

Charles Darwin thought that suspicion, along with the related emotion of jealousy, was impossible to portray in paintings because as a feeling that lasted for a prolonged period it was not characterized by anything as fleeting as a facial expression. James Stewart in *Rear Window* does his best to challenge that notion. The emotions he evokes range from frustration to indolent lust, but his dominant expression is the one shown in this photograph: narrowed eyes and intensely focused stare.

4b

Thwarted love is the overarching emotion of this scene, but something of each of these three moods might be on display. Having said a final goodbye to the love of her life, this woman is returning home to the husband for whom, as she only now realizes, she has never felt more than fondness. But perhaps there is also something more aggressive in the gaze: the bittersweet farewell has been interrupted by an airheaded acquaintance, and she is struggling to suppress her murderous impulses. She thinks in voiceover, "I wish you were dead—no, I don't mean that, that was silly and unkind." If you hadn't gathered already, this is the penultimate scene from *Brief Encounter*.

5b

These eyes are staring from the "sunken place" depicted in the 2017 film *Get Out*. The sunken place is a nightmarish metaphor for the sense of panic and despair caused by African Americans' experience of white aggression and attempts to erase their culture. The hero has just started to grasp that his white girlfriend's apparently accommodating family is hiding its predatory violence. Director Jordan Peele says that the conceit speaks to a range of experiences of disempowerment, from the literal (such as the mass incarceration of African American men) to the insidious: "You know when you're going to sleep and it feels like you're about to fall, so you wake up? What if you never woke up?"

6b

In the climactic moment of *Die Hard*, Bruce Willis's gunslinging hero cuts the suave terrorist Hans Gruber loose from the top storey of a Los Angeles skyscraper. The audience watches as he plunges to his doom—this is the face of a man in the split second he realizes that death is imminent. The expression of panic is real: the shot was captured as Alan Rickman was falling back in a 20-foot drop toward a blue pillow, an experience he says evoked "true terror."

7a

Here's yet another clip that captures the moment in which a person begins a fatal descent. But the emotions of this scene are very different to those expressed by Alan Rickman in *Die Hard*. In the film *Thelma and Louise*, following an exuberant road trip crime spree that began with the murder of a sexual predator, the two friends have finally run out of luck and are surrounded by police overlooking a canyon. It looks like the end of the line, but Louise has other ideas. "Let's keep going," she says, and, hands clasped, they drive off the cliff and into the sunset. It should be a tragic and horrifying finale, but the emotion of the scene is more exhilarating than sad: a moment of joy and friendship as they make their escape from a society marred by exploitation and brutality.

8c

"You see, that is just like you, Harry. You say things like that, and you make it impossible for me to hate you. And I hate you, Harry....I really hate you." Those are the words of Meg Ryan's character, Sally, in *When Harry Met Sally*, and perhaps some kind of hate is part of what she feels. But as the cliché goes, there's a thin line between love and hate: the next moment Harry and Sally are in each other's arms, decades of will-they-won't-they resolved into romantic catharsis.

Hokusai, facial expressions, early 19th century

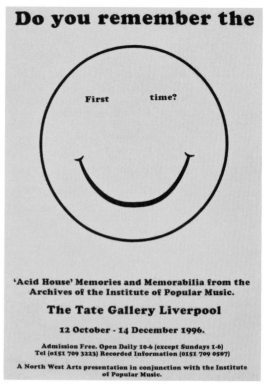

TOP LEFT: Artist unknown, Czechoslovakia, c. 1935 TOP RIGHT: Jeremy Deller, from series of posters, 1994–96
ABOVE: Jeremy Deller, *Don't Worry Be Angry*, 2017: "Pledge of Allegiance" (to being political),
commissioned by Creative Time / photo by NIcholas Prakas

THE PREHISTORY OF EMOJI

In 1982, a computer scientist named Scott Fahlman became frustrated with a recurrent problem he had noticed on his university message board. His colleagues, discovering online messaging for the first time, were continually falling into misunderstandings over comments intended in a lighthearted or ironic spirit. "I propose the following character sequence for joke markers: :-). Read it sideways," wrote Fahlman. "Actually, it is probably more economical to mark things that are NOT jokes, given current trends. For this, use :-(."

Fahlman's formula was even pithier than famously succinct equations like the mass–energy equivalence in special relativity ($e = mc^2$). And in its own more modest way, :-) sparked a revolution too: this is widely regarded as the moment the smiley was born. Fahlman's emoticons quickly migrated from the Carnegie Mellon University staff forum to message boards all over the embryonic internet.

As they proliferated, emoticons also mutated into an alphabet of crudely rendered cartoon expressions, each intended to convey a different emotional tone. Some, such as ;), :-o, or }:), were intuitive text-doodles. Others were more gnomic, like :-###.. (being sick) or XD (a laughing face).

As computer communication platforms became more flashy and elaborate, emoticons evolved into emoji. Surprisingly, the similarity between these two words is purely coincidental: the term *emoji* derives not from *emotions*, but from the Japanese phrase meaning "picture character" (the closest English equivalent is "ideogram"). But it's an apt coincidence. The Unicode Consortium, gatekeeper of the emoji lexicon, receives thousands of submissions for new emoji every year, and the capacity to express emotion is listed among the most important criteria for acceptance.

In 2020 there are over 3,000 emoji, with more added every year. Books have been published composed exclusively of emoji, including an emoji "translation" of Moby Dick and—to accusations of blasphemy—an emoji Bible. To this extent, emoji are not just signifiers of tone but an independent language.

So what are emoji? Are they a kind of minimalist pictorial art, like comic strips or cave paintings? Are they tonal markers, like an elaborate form of punctuation? Or are they a fluid, evolving language of their own?

There are two separate but related strands in the prehistory of emoji: the iconography of the smiling face and the many attempts to soften the uncompromising solidity of the printed word.

Much like exclamation or question marks, smileys are a way to translate onto the page the shifts in meaning and tone that in spoken language are conveyed by subtle shifts in tone, volume and body language: a raised brow, a fleeting frown, a raised voice, a questioning cadence or lilt.

In medieval Europe, when the idea of punctuation was relatively new, experimental symbols came and went. A rhetorical question, for instance, could be signaled by a reverse question mark. As printing became ubiquitous, writers started to toy with the idea of using printed characters to echo facial expressions. In 1881 *Puck* magazine came up with a series of punctuation portraits—*type-faces*, they might be called—in a playful attempt to put their illustrators out of business. In 1887 the American writer Ambrose Bierce proposed a new type of "punctuation": a horizontal bracket suggesting a smile for each "jocular or ironical sentence."

Joy.

Melancholy.

Indifference.

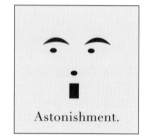
Astonishment.

While some toyed with old punctuation marks, others introduced new ones in an attempt to fill the gaps. The twentieth-century French poet Hervé Bazin suggested a set of mood markers, including the "irony point" (1), the "love point" (2), and the "doubt point" (3), while in 1962 the advertising executive Martin Speckter came up with an innovation that almost stuck. His writers had developed a habit of indicating surprised or sarcastic questions with both an exclamation and a question mark. Speckter's more elegant solution was the interrobang (4), which can still be found in many typefaces today.

1

2

3

4

The aesthetic of the modern emoji, with its default yellow; broad, dopey grin; and creased lips, is clearly a descendant of the acid house smiley of rave culture. But this image has a hidden heritage of its own: it was appropriated from a 1962 design, commissioned to boost the morale of employees at a Massachusetts insurance company.

Then came the internet. Suddenly huge crowds of strangers were chatting informally in text form. The puzzle of text and tone which had previously preoccupied poets and graphic designers became everyone's problem. Scott Fahlman made his fateful suggestion, and a thousand emoticons blossomed.

For the most part, emoji and emoticons have attempted to indicate a readily identifiable emotional category. A smile is reassuring, lighthearted, content; a frown is its opposite. But in the great proliferation of emoticons that followed the birth of the internet, some symbols convey an emotion that doesn't easily translate into our existing vocabulary. One example is the shruggie, otherwise known as the smugshrug: ¯_(ツ)_/¯. First composed by a young New Yorker trying to spice up her internet dating profile, the shruggie took on a life of its own when Kanye West appeared to make a similar gesture as he gazumped Taylor Swift at the Grammies. In this context it signified a lighthearted gloat: you've done something outrageous, but you're just too superior to care.

Subsequently, though, the shruggie has developed a very different meaning: a sort of bemused nihilistic acceptance amid the bewildering cascade of horrifying information that characterizes life on the internet—especially in an age of authoritarianism, climate catastrophe, and pandemics. As tech journalist Kevin Nguyen put it: "It was the ¯_(ツ)_/¯ of times, it was the ¯_(ツ)_/¯ of times."

From Charles Darwin's *The Expression of the Emotions in Man and Animals*, "Disgust," 1872

DISGUST CHRISTOPHER TURNER

His case history file identifies him only as NK. The patient had suffered a stroke at the age of twenty-five but experienced no loss of memory. His brain was for the most part apparently unimpaired, yet his stroke nevertheless had a curious effect: it altered his sense of disgust. He would sit down to eat a bowl of soup even after someone had stirred it with a flyswatter right in front of him. He happily devoured a piece of chocolate disguised as a dog turd. He slept soundly on the unwashed sheets of someone who had died the previous night. Andy Calder, a neuroscientist at Cambridge University who put NK through these disturbing tests, also showed his patient a series of pictures of people exhibiting different emotional expressions. NK named the emotions with ease—apart from disgust, which he incorrectly identified as sadness. Likewise, when played a soundtrack along a spectrum from laughter to retching, he was impaired only in recognizing the unpleasant vomiting noises. He could no longer, it seemed, process any social signals of disgust.

NK suffered from a rare neurological condition that makes the sufferer unable to recognize expressions of disgust in others, as well as making them immune to foul smells and tastes. MRI scans revealed that NK had damaged the deepest and oldest part of his brain—the insular cortex (brain surgeons had already noticed that stimulating the insula during surgery induced sensations of nausea in patients, who reported a foul taste in their mouths). For most people, disgust seems to be consistently provoked by blood, viscera, feces, sweat, slime, filth, sores, stench, rot, vermin, and putrefaction. The paradigm of the disgusting object is a corpse swarming with maggots: the uncanny appearance of life in something dead. Many suppose that disgust serves to protect us from things that threaten infection, disease, and ultimately death: among our ancestors, those who had a heightened sense of disgust gained an evolutionary advantage that has been handed down to us. In other words, disgust—that most primal of emotions—is in our genes, the result of millions of years of natural selection.

Charles Darwin was the first to study disgust empirically. His 1872 book *The Expression of the Emotions in Man and Animals* contains a chapter on disgust, which Darwin regarded as a core emotion—a departure from early typologies of the passions, in which disgust did not appear. Describing the expression of disgust, illustrated with histrionic photographs by Duchenne de Boulogne and the Victorian photographer Oscar Rejlander, Darwin focused almost exclusively on the mouth. He believed that the recoiling, retching expression exhibited in disgust was a relic of an earlier stage in hominid development when humans had the ability to vomit voluntarily, as he had observed monkeys doing in the London Zoo. Humans had lost this ability, Darwin thought, because they had replaced it with speech and were now able to warn others of contaminants in less visceral ways. He connected disgust with the interjections (Ugh! Pooh!) that he believed to be the origins of speech. For him this most primitive and visceral of the emotions was therefore the very foundation of language, and by extension of culture.

Sigmund Freud, the Austrian founder of psychoanalysis, was the principal scientific heir to Darwin's evolutionary belief that disgust is the emotion that defines us as human. Freud invented an elaborate prehistoric just-so story to explain how man first learned disgust when he first started to walk erect. Freud thought that our evolutionary ascent from all fours, which wrested the nose away from the excretory organs, was accompanied by a diminution of our olfactory powers and a corresponding horror of excrement and shame at the genitalia. The emotion of disgust, which every child learns through toilet training, polices the border between the pure and polluting, both reminding us of our earlier animal condition and preventing us from reverting to that state. However, Freud asserts, the repressed always returns to worry culture, which explains the secret, nihilistic, powerful attraction of the disgusting. Immanuel Kant remarked of this paradoxical magnetism that the disgusting "insists on being enjoyed."

The Hungarian phenomenologist Aurel Kolnai elaborates on this unconscious desire: "There is an element of invitation in disgust. I might say a lure, an enticement…but the invitation actualises the defence." We can't resist sneaking a rubbernecking glance at the disgusting, in all its glistening putrescence, its violence and horror, before we turn away gagging and retching. It seems almost as if the nasty tastes, smells or sights have already been absorbed, which is why they provoke violent vomiting as the stomach (and mind) tries to turn the intruder out. Many avant-garde artists have sought to exploit such psychic ambivalence, seeing something cathartic and redemptive in disgust. The Dadaists (who included a section in their manifesto on "Dadaist disgust") and Surrealists (dubbed "excrementalists" by some detractors) mobilized disgust as a radical and critical force in their assault on the bourgeois values and culture that they saw as a sickness that culminated in the First World War. Existentialist philosophers such as Jean-Paul Sartre followed them in thinking that the shock and nausea that disgust provokes was a stimulus to revolution; by confronting us with the meaninglessness of existence and putting everything in flux, it invites us to question our values and invent a new world.

Later theorists such as William Ian Miller and Martha Nussbaum have argued that disgust is a fundamentally conservative emotion in that, when extended to moral as well as physical contaminants, it serves to reinforce the status quo—the caste system in India is maintained by disgust, as was the rhetoric of anti-Semitism in Nazi Germany that saw Freud exiled, and is the aggressive language of homophobia. Of course, others exhibit moral repugnance at those same things. Disgust—which threatens the breakdown of the distinction between subject and object and the erosion of other symbolic boundaries—is an emotion characterized by extreme ambivalence. Maybe only NK, whose stroke-damaged brain had seemingly transcended disgust, an emotion that Darwin and Freud thought defined us as human, was free of all the antisocial elements of a passion that also serves to divide us.

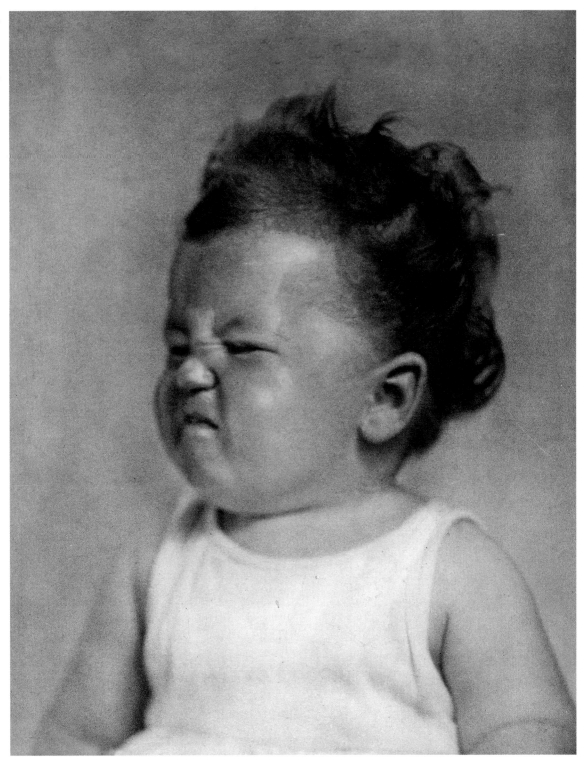

"What on Earth have you been putting in these cakes?" Photograph from an advertisement for Melhuish's New Harvest Flour, c. 1932

Sam Taylor-Johnson, *Willem Dafoe* from the *Crying Men* series, 2002–04

RELATIONSHIPS

ZELDA FITZGERALD TO SCOTT

Dearest–

It seemed very sad to see you going off in your new shoes alone. Little human vanities are somehow the most moving poignant things in people you love—Struggles and deep emotions when you are closely identified with are apt to assume the unconscious epic quality but the little things about people are always so touching—

Darling, darling I love you so—To-day seems like Easter, and I wish we were together walking slow thru the sunshine and the crowds from Church—Everything smells so good and warm, and your ring shines so white in the sun—like one of the church lillies with a little yellow dust on it—We ought to be together [in] the Spring—it seems made for us to love in—

From *Dear Scott, Dearest Zelda: The Love Letters of F. Scott and Zelda Fitzgerald*, 2003

A LOVE SPELL...AND ITS ANTIDOTE

Love is generally thought of as the most ungovernable of emotions: it falls on us suddenly like an anvil from an empty sky and leaves us blissfully helpless to resist. According to a 1997 study, falling in love is so prosaically scientific that anybody can do it in just a few minutes by following a simple thirty-six-step script.

The following questions are lifted directly from this study. They are not just a game but the material for a peer-reviewed psychological study. Try it, if you dare. Find a partner and get close to them—don't touch, but stare into each other's eyes without breaking contact. Then ask each other the following questions and answer them as honestly as you possibly can. If a couple of hours have passed and you haven't eloped, perhaps true love is more elusive than the research suggests...

36 QUESTIONS TO FALL IN LOVE

SET I

1. Given the choice of anyone in the world, whom would you want as a dinner guest?

2. Would you like to be famous? In what way?

3. Before making a telephone call, do you ever rehearse what you are going to say? Why?

4. What would constitute a perfect day for you?

5. When did you last sing to yourself? To someone else?

6. If you were able to live to the age of ninety and retain either the mind or body of a thirty-year-old for the last sixty years of your life, which would you want?

7. Do you have a secret hunch about how you will die?

8. Name three things you and your partner appear to have in common.

9. For what in your life do you feel most grateful?

10. If you could change anything about the way you were raised, what would it be?

11. Take four minutes and tell your partner your life story in as much detail as possible.

12. If you could wake up tomorrow having gained any one quality or ability, what would it be?

SET 2

13. If a crystal ball could tell you the truth about yourself, your life, the future, or anything else, what would you want to know?

14. Is there something that you've dreamed of doing for a long time? Why haven't you done it?

15. What is the greatest accomplishment of your life?

16. What do you value most in a friendship?

17. What is your most treasured memory?

18. What is your most terrible memory?

19. If you knew that in one year you would die suddenly, would you change anything about the way you are now living? Why?

20. What does friendship mean to you?

21. What roles do love and affection play in your life?

22. Alternate sharing something you consider a positive characteristic of your partner. Share a total of five items.

23. How close and warm is your family? Do you feel your childhood was happier than most other people's?

24. How do you feel about your relationship with your mother?

SET 3

25. Make three true "we" statements each. For instance, "We are both in this room feeling..."

26. Complete this sentence: "I wish I had someone with whom I could share..."

27. If you were going to become a close friend with your partner, please share what would be important for them to know.

28. Tell your partner what you like about them; be very honest this time, saying things that you might not say to someone you've just met.

29. Share with your partner an embarrassing moment in your life.

30. When did you last cry in front of another person? By yourself?

31. Tell your partner something that you like about them already.

32. What, if anything, is too serious to be joked about?

33. If you were to die this evening with no opportunity to communicate with anyone, what would you most regret not having told someone? Why haven't you told them yet?

34. Your house, containing everything you own, catches fire. After saving your loved ones and pets, you have time to safely make a final dash to save any one item. What would it be? Why?

35. Of all the people in your family, whose death would you find most disturbing? Why?

36. Share a personal problem and ask your partner's advice on how they might handle it. Also, ask your partner to reflect back to you how you seem to be feeling about the problem you have chosen.

Illustration from a comic, USA, c. 1960

Perhaps you have made the mistake of undertaking the exercise above with a totally inappropriate partner, leaving you infatuated and miserable. Perhaps you are having a passionate affair with a coworker and desperately need it to stop before things get out of hand. Or perhaps you are so certain of your unbreakable bond that you are willing to put it to the ultimate test. Whatever your reasons, these nineteen steps are guaranteed to end your love affair.

Instructions: Stare into your partner's eyes and assume a look of bored contempt. Then take turns in asking the questions below, each answering them as honestly as you can..

(Disclaimer: unlike the previous list, these questions have no basis in psychological research.)

1. If you could burn one possession of mine, what would it be?
2. Which of my family members do you find most unbearable?
3. Which friend of mine do you falsely pretend to like?
4. Which friend of mine do you like more than you really should?
5. Imagine we were both kidnapped by a sadistic murderer who vowed to kill one of us, and made us decide which it would be. Which of us would go free and which would end up being murdered?
6. What quality do I most overrate in myself? Is there something I'm proud of with no good reason?
7. Describe, in detail, an unconscious tic of mine that drives you to distraction.
8. Tell me something you've always wanted to say to me but never dared.
9. What's something you know about me that I don't know that you know?
10. What has most disappointed you about me?
11. When was the last time you were angry with me but decided not to let it show?
12. What dreams and ambitions has our relationship prevented you from fulfilling?
13. What would you most like to change about my appearance?
14. Which of your previous partners do you most miss and what did they give you that I can't?
15. What's something you could truthfully say about yourself that would genuinely shock me?
16. What film or book that I like have you pretended to like?
17. Which of us works hardest on our relationship—financially, emotionally, in terms of day-to-day chores?
18. Describe all the ways in which your life would have been better if we had never met.
19. When was the last time you were ashamed to be associated with me?

If you made it this far and still want to spend the evening together, well done—either it's true love, or you're good enough at lying to each other that it might as well be.

THE OVERACTIVE EMPATHY TEST

What's going on in these pictures?

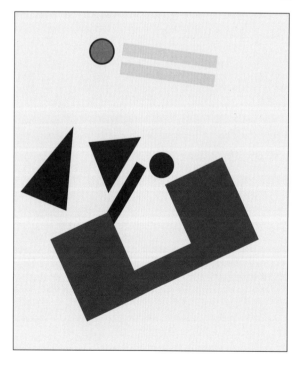

Perhaps you saw this as the story of two angry triangles hunting down a square, then hiding shame-faced after committing some sort of indiscretion before making a dash for safety. Perhaps the two triangles are fighting over the square. Perhaps it's a story about the interior psychodrama of the whole shape-complex at the bottom of the screen: an emotionally closed mind that gradually opens up to the world, timidly at first and then with more confidence—only to discover that it is still vulnerable to the triangles of self-doubt. Perhaps you saw a completely different narrative unfold (what does the enigmatic, unassuming green circle in the top left indicate?).

Or maybe you saw nothing at all.

These abstract graphics are based on a psychological experiment designed by Fritz Heider and Marianne Simmel. Subjects were shown a short film featuring a series of shapes floating around on a screen, without any predetermined logic. Almost all of them interpreted the shapes as animate objects, individuals with intentions, feelings, and relationships, interacting in complicated ways.

If you trust the results of the experiment, it seems as though people are capable of seeing emotional intentions in literally anything. This tendency to project might be one reason why we often misread the emotional lives of our nearest and dearest,

EMOTIONAL LABOR

Grete Stern, *Dream 15*, 1949

From the *Naya-nayika* set of lovers' quarrels, India, 19th century

In 1983 the sociologist Arlie Hochschild called attention to an unsettling phenomenon that she had noticed among the flight attendants whose working conditions she had been researching for several years. The airline seemed less concerned about training in practical duties than about ensuring that its hospitality staff project a consistently serene and sympathetic persona—and the psychological demands of this performance were taking their toll. "Sometimes I come home from a long trip in a state of utter exhaustion," said one young trainee, "but I find I can't relax. I giggle a lot, I chatter, I call friends. It's as if I can't release myself from an artificially created elation that kept me 'up' on the trip."

This sense of alienation from their own feelings was a result of the particular emotional techniques that flight attendants were encouraged to use. It wasn't enough merely to act as though they were chirpy and serene; they were also supposed to feel all of the emotions that they performed. If a passenger was grouchy or disruptive, the flight attendant was instructed to empathize with his mood (the attendants were almost always female, and the hypothetical passengers generally men). Instead of growing angry with him, the attendants were to "think about the other person and why they're so upset"—even, the instructor suggested, imagining that "his son had just died." Instead of suppressing their irritation at the obnoxious passenger, they would commit themselves to service with even deeper sympathy and devotion. "Our smiles are not just painted on" was more than a jingle on the PA system.

To describe this phenomenon, Hochschild coined a new term: emotional labor. Workers in such emotionally demanding jobs, she said, were alienated from their inner lives: instead of reflecting their own moods, their feelings were co-opted in service to their employers. They were feeling on behalf of other people or even of corporations—and in the process losing touch with their own sense of self.

It's not just flight attendants who are expected to strenuously manage their emotional states. Waitresses face similar demands, although in a less intense situation. Childcare workers are supposed to be bubbly and energetic, even when they are screaming inside. According to the original definition of emotional labor, bouncers, police officers, and tax collectors must all perform it, with the roles reversed: rather than a cheery demeanor, they may be required to suppress sympathy, put on a hostile front, and exude confidence or anger in the face of desperate people pleading for clemency.

If emotional labor is understood as alienation from one's feelings, then both suppressing and performing empathy are examples of that phenomenon. In more recent years, the term has become more exclusively associated with the sort of female-coded work typified by the original example of flight attendants. Even in its original context, the idea was closely tied to structural inequalities and expectations of gender roles: the jobs that most clearly require the enactment of a particular persona are service industry professions dominated by women. Many of these jobs come with low status and low pay, despite their exacting emotional demands. Despite the deep emotional and mental resources that such workers are required to draw on, their effort is undervalued and belittled because it is understood as "women's work."

More recently, the term has taken on broader feminist applications. First, it has been used to describe the social and emotional functions foisted on women in the workplace, regardless of whether they work in jobs that make specific emotional demands. Who keeps the office community thrumming along with encouragement and friendly conversation? Who organizes after-work drinks and ensures meetings don't descend into grandstanding and tiffs? This scarcely recognized and often draining labor overwhelmingly falls to women. What is more, it places women in professional positions in a double bind: whether to be emotionally available and accept the extra burden or to be judged as cold and unfeeling.

In these examples, emotional labor occurs in the context of paid work. But unpaid domestic labor overwhelmingly falls on the shoulders of women. In the UK, for example, the average woman in a heterosexual relationship does sixteen hours of household chores each week, while the average man does six. Hochschild wrote a book on this, too, and coined yet another term that has spread beyond the boundaries of academic writing: the "second shift." Like the formal first shift, this unofficial second job requires women to be constantly mentally and emotionally vigilant.

A 2005 study showed that women spent far more time than men emotionally supporting their families and that this role required effort, focus, and management. The researchers called for an expansion of the definition of "housework" to include this intangible nurture and care. An essay published in *Harper's Bazaar* struck a powerful chord with its descriptions of the emotional exhaustion felt by women who work in draining full-time jobs only to return home to a barrage of further demands on their time, empathy, and logistical dexterity. Women tend to bear the brunt not only of cooking and cleaning but also of meal planning, social calendars, and emotional support. And this churn of tasks carries a psychological burden: from anxiety at the ever-growing to-do list to guilt at failure to meet the impossible standards inscribed by normative gender roles.

Critics of the idea of emotional labor often say that it is dehumanizing to think about care and compassion as transactional work. But perhaps that is exactly the problem—as Hochschild says: "The solution is not for men and women to share alienated work. The solution is for men and women to share enchanted work." The idea that our personal and domestic duties could be illuminated by a sense of agency and authentic desire offers some hope of a better way of relating to one another.

AFTER THE PARTY

NATALIE HUME

So Darling, you know what I mentioned to you the other day, about each of us contributing to all aspects of our wonderful life together? You know, some people call it emotional labor—ring any bells? I wasn't sure if you were listening—sometimes it's hard to tell. Anyway, I just wanted to catch up with you about all…that. Because—this is such a trivial thing, really, but—I thought it was a bit insensitive that you didn't even pretend to know what was in Jack's present that was supposed to be from both of us. I thought perhaps you could just have raised a knowing eyebrow or something instead of looking bewildered. You claimed not to remember it was his birthday, but actually it's been in our diary for months. It's not exactly a forgettable date anyway…How can you not remember April Fools' Day? We make the same jokes every year. It doesn't matter, of course. It's just that then you left me to organize the seating, which was quite complicated. As you know, Erica and Jane detest each other, and Steven has to be kept away from Amelie because he still hasn't got over her and he almost didn't come at all. I persuaded him by saying we'd be devastated if he wasn't there, and you barely spoke to him, so he kept looking at me as though I'd made it all up. So I was trying to figure out where everyone could sit, and I still didn't know if that awful friend of yours was coming, and the cat had been sick under the table, and I didn't know whether to try to clean it up without anyone seeing or make a joke of it—the smell seemed so awful. Then Stella woke up and said she wanted you, but you were smoking in the garden with Alastair, so I had to let her watch a film on my laptop. I know we don't want to ruin her sleep schedule, but Darling, it's just impossible if you're never around to help. Then there was the crisis with Tom! You know I always put almonds in my chocolate torte, and he claimed as he left for the ER that he'd told you he was allergic. Honestly, Darling, he could have died and it would have been all my fault! The absolute worst thing was the lobsters. You said you'd be in charge and it would be like putting them in a lovely warm bath and they'd fall asleep without realizing, but you left me with them and it was too ghastly—they escaped, and I was rushing round the kitchen after them and the elastic bands came off their claws and I had to hit them with a rolling pin. They were so frightening but also terribly pathetic, and now I keep having nightmares about them. To tell you the truth, I don't think I can ever do a dinner party again and actually I'm not sure I want to live with you anymore—oh dear, I'm so sorry! I do hope you'll be OK.

Blue lobster from *Dictionnaire universel d'histoire naturelle*, 1892

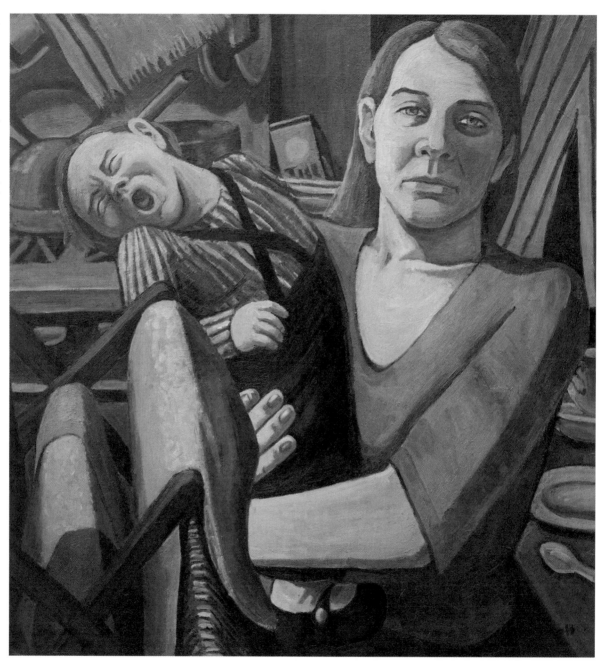

Maureen Scott, *Mother and Child at Breaking Point*, 1970

TRANSMISSIONS FROM THE UNCONSCIOUS

ROSE DEMPSEY

A familiar scene: we are standing in the queue at the shops when a mother joins us with a baby in a stroller. The baby awakes and is immediately in the throes of a screaming rage: arms and legs writhing, head twisted, face puce, as if confronted with the threat of its own annihilation. The mother desperately tries to soothe the wild creature. The commotion registers somewhere deep within us bystanders. What terrible misfortune has befallen this innocent child? Should we step in and help? Do we want to rescue the baby or smother it?

One of the most powerful and important insights from psychoanalysis is that some version of this screaming child lives within all of us. Its fears, its desires, its frustrations and insecurities echo throughout our adult lives. It is impossible to get through childhood unscathed; we may develop sophisticated defenses against the reopening of these early wounds, but these defenses shape our behaviors and relationships in unwanted ways.

Freud's model of the unconscious mind revealed a turmoil lurking behind our everyday conscious states: ideas and sensations vying for expression but held back through repression. Over the past century, psychoanalysts have developed a rich language for the deflections and distortions we perform unconsciously in order to protect ourselves from these primal states of mind.

Transference: Spreading the love (and anger, guilt, fear…)

During therapy, a patient unearthing buried feelings toward a parental figure might disconcertingly start to experience those same feelings, directed at the therapist: love, perhaps, but also resentment, bitterness, or betrayal. This *transference* is not only accepted but expected: it's fundamental to the therapeutic process, an essential way of confronting suppressed emotion.

But transference is a powerful force far beyond the consulting room. A partner doesn't reply to a text for a few hours, and you feel hopelessly abandoned; your manager casually rejects your suggestion in a meeting, and you are momentarily filled with inordinate rage; on having to cancel a trivial social engagement, you are consumed with debilitating guilt. Perhaps your feelings are not about these humdrum disappointments in your day-to-day life but about forgotten events in your childhood, when your half-understood, overwhelmingly vivid world was thrown into chaos by the behavior of a carer or companion.

Transference can be exploited by authority figures, for purposes sinister or benign. At work, employees are often encouraged to idealize bosses, a positive transference in aid of greater productivity that evokes the parental relationship. Dictators rely on a similar mass transference, presenting themselves as fathers of the nation as they mete out discipline in the guise of supervision and care.

Projection and identification: whose feelings are these, anyway?

Projection is one of our most recognizable defense mechanisms. Unable to bear difficult feelings such as envy or greed, we split them off and ascribe them to someone else: the playground bully wants his victim to feel the fear and anxiety that he himself is experiencing elsewhere. The projection president Donald Trump responds to criticism by lobbying identical charges at his opponents. "Lock her up," says the man whose career is blighted by the whiff of corruption and criminality.

Projection and transference can take an even more sinister turn. Haunted by an emotion that she can neither suppress nor confront, a person with a powerful personality might find ways to offload her corrosive emotions into somebody else's psyche. It's a survival mechanism with unsettling consequences: as we absorb these affects and begin to take on characteristics transmitted to us in this way, we are likely to lose our sense of autonomy and become alienated from ourselves.

The shadow self

Shakespeare's Othello is an uncommonly eloquent and self-possessed man whose behavior is exemplary toward all around him, despite the resentment many of his companions feel about him. When he turns on his beloved Desdemona and murders her, is he really acting from something so simple as sexual jealousy? Or does this moment represent the cracking of a carefully built facade, revealing all the ugly feelings he has suppressed? According to the Swiss psychoanalyst Carl Jung, we each have a "shadow self" into which we pour all the qualities that we are desperate to hide from the outside world. In a situation of extreme stress, this hidden monster might emerge.

The false self and the "good enough" mother

The postwar British psychologist Donald Winnicott did not see the relationship between the carer and her child as one of bland harmony: no parent can sustain the devotion to fulfill a child's bottomless demands for sustenance and love. He developed the concept of the "good enough" mother: a figure who gives the child what it needs—but not always as much or as instantly as it demands. In the resulting struggle, the baby learns to assert itself in a world of competing wills: it must accept that the mother is a separate entity, not just a source of limitless praise. "The normal child," Winnicott wrote, "pulls out all the stops. In the course of time, he tries out his power to disrupt, to destroy, to frighten, to wear down, to waste, to wangle, and to appropriate."

The emerging human is messy, sometimes obnoxious—but also authentic and independent. Sometimes, however, this tempestuous normality is suppressed because of overcompliance. In cases like this, a false self emerges: an outwardly good personality that masks an inner emptiness. Goodness has subsumed the self.

Rage and reverie: the drama of the breast

In the Austrian-British psychoanalyst Melanie Klein's version, the setting for the melodrama between carer and child is the mother's breast. The primal need for food, if not immediately met, fills the baby with destructive rage: the magical object that provides it with the means to live is withholding the food, presumably for itself. It is an interplay of fear and desire, envy and gratitude, love and rage.

What is the baby's carer to make of all this? The British psychoanalyst Wilfred Bion described the maternal "reverie": a calm, attentive state in which the mother can enter the baby's mind and experience its emotions and needs. She receives the projected feelings willingly and projects them back in a safe form. In this wordless exchange the baby might learn how to experience its bewildering passions safely.

Think back to the screaming child in the shop. The child's tantrum is its first attempt to communicate feelings and assert itself. But it is not the only character in this psychodrama. The mother, subjected to an onslaught of projected emotions, is caught up in the storm, and her reaction in turn is shaped by similar early emotional experiences, the results of which she is still living with. Meanwhile, we, the bystanders, absorb this torrent of affect while reexperiencing our own ambivalent feelings. Hidden in the glare of the strip lighting is a glimpse of the network of wordless transference, projection, and identification that silently structures our interlocking emotional worlds.

Piero della Francesca, *Madonna of Mercy*, central panel from the Misericordia Altarpiece, 1460–62

4

CULTURES OF EMOTION

LOST AND FOUND

Do you ever have a feeling that you can't quite find the right word for? Perhaps that's because the word you're trying to think of doesn't exist. But that's not to say that it never did. Over the course of history, the language of feeling has been in constant flux. New words have come into being, often borrowed from science, philosophy, and theology, to describe emotional states that were previously unnamed. Our sentimental lexicon retains the flotsam from countless discarded ideas about the nature of emotions, while new terms are constantly added to the inventory.

While the general tendency of our emotional vocabulary is toward constant expansion and elaboration, some emotions have fallen out of favor. Do these lost emotions continue to exist in a ghostly state, floating nameless in our collective psyche? Or does the fact that we have no language for them suggest that they are no longer truly felt? And what about the found emotions? Are we discovering new feelings that were nesting unnoticed in our subconscious? Or are we inventing emotions that have never existed before? Here are a few of the emotions from the remainder box of history.

LOST: ACEDIA

Picture yourself as a sixth-century Christian monk in a monastery in the middle of the Sahara. Every day of your life is devoted to the study and worship of God. Life is austere, but the contemplation of the divine offers you all the fulfillment and sense of meaning you could possibly want. It is both your duty and your overriding passion, and it is more than enough.

Except, that is, on certain barren afternoons, when the hot wind blows in and with it a draining sense of lethargy. Suddenly, all of your awe and reverence drains away. You can't bring yourself to care about God, or the world, or anything at all—even the very apathy that is draining your faith and your will. You drift listlessly through the day, staring at the sun as it creeps across the sky. You are bereft.

This state of overpowering ennui is *acedia*, known among the Desert Fathers as the "midday demon." Before there were seven sins there were eight principal vices—ungodly urges that could corrupt even the most devout worshipper—and acedia was among them. Some believed that it was swept in on the breeze by a malevolent spirit; what was certain was that it was one of the greatest threats to spiritual safety that a dedicated Christian could face. It was understood as a sort of unadulterated worldliness, a total alienation from God.

The phenomenon of an afternoon slump remains familiar enough, even to those of us not subject to desert winds. Modern scientists tend to explain it in far less daunting terms: as a quirk of our circadian rhythms or a side effect of a carb-heavy diet. While we might be able to empathize with those monks, you may not truly feel acedia unless you ascribe similarly dire spiritual meanings to your daily torpor.

Pieter Bruegel the Elder, *Acedia*, 1558

Unknown photographer, 1960s

FOUND: STRESS

It sometimes feels as though the entire condition of twenty-first-century life can be summed up by this one word. Too much work, too many emails, too much news in too many browser tabs and too few hours in the day. We sleep too little, drink too much, and never have fewer than eight things on our mind at once. In a word, we are stressed.

Stress may or may not be *the* modern condition, but it certainly is *a* modern condition: the now-ubiquitous term was adopted to describe a mental state around 1936. Conducting experiments on rats, the psychologist Hans Selye realized that his subjects were suffering effects that could not be explained by the cocktail of hormones and drugs they had been given. He developed a theory that the rats' illnesses and deaths were in fact a consequence of the experiments themselves. From this observation he developed a three-stage model of stress: confronted with an alarming situation, we first struggle against it, then attempt to accommodate ourselves within it. Sometimes neither of these tactics work. In this case, we reach the stage of "exhaustion" and collapse—or perhaps even die.

In the decades after the Second World War, researchers ascribed an increasing number of physical and mental health conditions to stress: cancer, depression, the common cold. Medical research suggested that the body was literally under physical strain. The term "stress" went from science to the newspaper pages to everyday speech, and pretty soon it was everywhere. In the US in 2017, three-quarters of people reported regular symptoms of serious stress. Almost a third lost sleep because of it. The cause is often banal: 62 percent of people are stressed about money and 61 percent about work—that is timeless, perhaps. But the most widespread cause of American stress speaks more to the spirit of our time: almost two-thirds of people are seriously stressed about the news.

LOST: DYSPEPSIA

In Victorian novels, it's common to find a character (usually male) described as "dyspeptic." Look up this word in the dictionary and you'll find that it's a medical term for indigestion, slightly archaic but still in use. Why, then, were many writers so eager to inform their readership of a character's stomach troubles as though they were a primary personality trait rather than a private irritation?

The reason is that both doctors and the public believed a troublesome gut to be inseparably associated with a particular kind of temperament: grouchy, embittered, quick to anger. Dyspepsia was an emotional state as much as an illness, and it was far from clear whether the feeling or the physiological condition came first: did a bad temper arise from the intestines, or was the gut suffering from festering bitterness of mind?

Interest in what is now known as the gut–brain axis has revived in recent years. Scientists have identified a dense neural network connecting the digestive system to the brain, suggesting that our food and our feelings are linked in direct and powerful ways. Perhaps it is time for dyspepsia to reenter our emotional lexicon.

FOUND: INSECURITY

This word is a key feature of our emotional vocabulary and even our understanding of character. "They're probably just insecure," we might say of a person whose behavior has been rude or selfish. But until very recently the idea of insecurity was associated more with bridges than human beings. That changed only with twentieth-century psychology, particularly with the attachment theory pioneered by John Bowlby and Harry Harlow.

Harlow's big idea was that our personalities are forged at our mother's breasts and that the reliability of our bonds with a mother figure can determine the entire course of our characters and lives. Harlow made this breakthrough during experiments using baby monkeys that had been removed from their mother. They would receive either no surrogate, a basic dummy (essentially a plank with a milk dispenser), or a more deluxe dummy with soothing fur. Even a fairly rudimentary dummy seemed to give the babies the stability they needed to grow into well-adjusted members of the monkey community. Without a stand-in mother, the orphaned monkeys grew up to have serious emotional problems: their attachment was insecure. It is this sort of experiment that lies at the root of our go-to excuse and consolation for the behavior of bullies and jerks.

LOST: MELANCHOLIA

Everyone knows what melancholy means, right? It's just sadness for poets. But the original melancholia was a different thing altogether. Renaissance melancholics were victims of the "glass delusion"—an unshakable conviction that your body might at any moment shatter like glass. Among those who suffered from this extreme sense of vulnerability was King Charles VI of France, who insisted that his body be constantly encased in metal armor lest it disintegrate on impact with the outside world.

Though this fantasy could manifest in other ways, it always related to a fundamental distrust in the physical integrity of the sufferer's body. Examples listed in Robert Burton's *Anatomy of Melancholy* include one man's terror that his head would fall off alongside another's morbid certainty that his belly was full of frogs. As far as it's possible for us to tell at such historical distance, the delusions of early melancholics weren't just lyrical descriptions of mental unrest: they literally felt they were made of glass. Although melancholia is often treated as an archaic term for depression, many of these earlier descriptions seem to have more in common with the modern concept of anxiety. The boundaries of emotional pathologies are constantly in flux, since they involve judgments about the socially prescribed limits of propriety and health.

FOUND: FOMO

"I should have gone home before midnight—I knew I had to get up to work. But I had such FOMO that I ended up staying until four." The dreaded fear of missing out sometimes seems like one of the most powerful motivating factors shaping modern lives. The basic impulse is as old as time. It's why we linger over a menu, dreading the possibility that our companion will end up with the more appetizing dish.

But with the birth of social media and the newly unlimited capacity to see our lives in the contexts of those of our peers, this urge to think in comparisons and counterfactuals has taken on monstrous proportions. So perhaps it's not surprising that it has finally been given a specific name.

LOST: NOSTALGIA

"Returning home," c. 1960

In 1830s Paris, on the rue de la Harpe, not far from Notre-Dame, there lived a simple, home-loving man whose thoroughly domestic routine was interrupted only by occasional trips to the flower market. His clean, orderly apartment was his greatest source of joy and pride. So when he was informed by his landlord one day that the building was scheduled for demolition, he was so bereft that he took to his bed and refused to leave the flat. When the dreaded day arrived, the landlord forced open the door and found him dead, "suffocated from the despair of having to leave the abode he cherished too much." The verdict: death by nostalgia.

The word had been invented a century and a half earlier, in 1688, by a Swiss medical student called Johannes Hofer. During his studies, he noticed a phenomenon among young conscripts billeted overseas: far removed from the familiar rhythms of their former Alpine village life, they would become anxious and unsettled, losing sleep and appetite to a life-threatening extent. Hofer labeled this condition "nostalgia," an amalgam of the Greek words *nostos* (home) and *algos* (suffering), in imitation of the existing German word *Heimweh*. The term caught on and took on meanings all of its own.

Over the following two centuries, "nostalgia" became a recognized term for a serious medical condition. All those who had been torn from their accustomed environments were at risk—children sent away to school, women in domestic service—but among soldiers it could take on the character of an epidemic. During the American Civil War, for instance, over 5,000 cases of nostalgia were registered among Union soldiers, and seventy-four deaths were recorded. Treatments ranged from leeches to hypnosis. Cases like this still occasionally turned up on casualty lists in the First World War. The individual circumstances of these deaths are obscure, but it is easy to imagine an eighteen-year-old from a small village pining away in the trenches of Ypres.

Since then, the word has lost some of its potency. Has modernity accustomed us to the expectation of constant novelty, eroding our dependence on familiar traditions and experiences? Perhaps. Nostalgia ain't what it used to be: like many terms in our emotional category, its meaning has slowly been softened, from a life-threatening pathology into a fairly everyday feeling that might even be a pleasurable indulgence. "I prefer the mystic clouds of nostalgia to the real thing," as the English folk musician Robert Wyatt confessed.

FOUND: COMPERSION

Sexual and romantic jealousy is seemingly one of the greatest constants in human history. It's the emotional crux of stories stretching back to *The Iliad* and beyond, and it's often held responsible for the entire apparatus of traditional gender and family structures: What is marriage for if not to suppress the ruinous potential of sexual rivalry? And it's not just confined to humans. Watch any David Attenborough–fronted nature program and you're likely to see a parade of raging mammals pummeling their chests in an attempt to assert their exclusive mating rights.

According to people in less conventional relationship models, however, jealousy is not the unconquerably primal passion that we often take it to be. Instead, it is a learned response born of a patriarchal culture in which love and sex are inextricably bound up with proprietorial urges. What if instead of wanting our lover all to ourselves, we could feel liberated and excited by their sexual adventures as well as our own?

Since the 1970s polyamorists have been using the term "compersion" to describe a feeling of vicarious joy at a partner being intimate with another person. According to its advocates, this emotion is something that everyone can cultivate in themselves: we simply need to unlearn the jealousy that has been instilled in us by a repressive system of sexual relations.

Found photograph, c. 1968

LOST: SENSIBILITY

Sweet SENSIBILITY! thou keen delight! / Unprompted moral! sullen sense of light!

Perception exquisite! fair virtue's seed! / Thou quick precursor of the lib'ral deed!

...To those who know thee not no words can paint, / And those who know thee, know all words are faint.

This is just one fragment of an extended rhapsody to the marvels of sensibility by the writer and philanthropist Hannah More in 1782. But what exactly was this quality that she so admired?

In the eighteenth century, being sensible did not necessarily imply that a person was reasonable and levelheaded. Instead, it indicated having an acute sensitivity to beauty and virtue or squalor and sin. A person of sensibility was always open to the influences of their environment, never hardening their spirit to the ugliness and injustice of the world: a man of feeling might weep upon witnessing an act of charity or blush and sigh uncontrollably at the sight of a beautiful woman. In fact, there are novels of the period, such as those of Laurence Sterne, in which entire conversations are carried out by the exclusive medium of blushes, sighs, and spasmodic gestures that reveal a turmoil of stirrings beneath the polite facade of bourgeois conversation: no need for verbal communication at all.

Sensibility is not so much a lost emotion as an entire set of beliefs about what emotions are, what they mean, and what they do. It was more than just a fashion for sensitivity and warmth: according to the likes of Hannah More, it was a matter not only of aesthetic refinement but also the source of all morality. For instance, the culture of sensibility had a huge impact on the emergence of abolitionism, of which More was a key advocate.

By the end of the eighteenth century, attitudes to sensibility had started to sour. By the time Jane Austen wrote *Sense and Sensibility*, she was portraying it as a qualified rather than an absolute virtue: refined feelings were important, but they needed to be tempered by practicality and caution or else they would leave you, like the romantic and impulsive Marianne Dashwood, at the mercy of irresponsible rogues and your own thoughtless whims. Within a few decades, sensibility was regularly being discussed as a kind of emotional frailty, even perhaps a disease.

What put an end to this emotional regime? Historians have blamed the French Revolution, among other things: when political passions overflowed into bloody rebellion and bloodier retribution, a fearful aristocracy became suspicious of where unfettered self-expression might lead. The famous Victorian policing of feeling that still influences British culture today was in part a result of this backlash against sensibility.

FOUND: BOREDOM

The first recorded instance of the word "boredom" did not occur until the nineteenth century. One of the earliest appears in Charles Dickens's *Bleak House*, identified as a "chronic malady" of the haughty, haunted Lady Dedlock.

Discussions of restlessness and monotony—including the aforementioned acedia—can be found in writing stretching back to ancient Greece and beyond. But some commentators have identified a certain significance in the sudden popularity of the term "boredom" in the age of Dickens. With the Industrial Revolution and the spread of mechanical timekeeping, the rhythms of the day had been increasingly divided into segments of work and leisure. For the first time in history, millions of people had stretches of the day that could be understood as free time—as distinct from the hours that were not truly theirs but belonged instead to their employers.

This sense of empty, purposeless time seemed dangerous to some: if it wasn't filled with self-improving activity, dangerous habits might emerge. So the new threat of boredom was combated with activities like botany, cycling, or team sports.

In our own age of ever-available overstimulation, there is a growing movement to rehabilitate the reputation of boredom. In London there is now an annual Boring Conference addressing subjects such as "inkjet printers of 1999." Some psychologists and sociologists suggest that uninvigorating activities that allow the mind to wander are a crucial precondition for creativity and independent thought.

FOUND: EMBARRASSMENT

For a lot of people (especially in self-conscious Britain) this is one of those everyday feelings that form the basic currency of social interactions. But although it is related to the nearly universally recognized *shame*, the idea of *embarrassment* is actually quite particular to English—and also relatively new. It evolved in the eighteenth century out of a word denoting physical blockage—the hampering or hindering of movement. Gradually this meaning was expanded and abstracted until it described an encumbrance to the steady flow of communication.

The word emerged during an era when the middle class was becoming porous, with the British Empire and Industrial Revolution providing an avenue to new wealth. This put a premium on refinement, wit, and decorum as ways of demonstrating that you truly belonged in polite society—unlike those dreadful parvenus. A misunderstanding, a misplaced remark, or an inappropriate joke suggested that the speaker was a kind of impostor. Conversation between cultivated equals ought to flow freely according to a prescribed set of rules. If it was blocked, that reflected on the speaker.

Embarrassment feels like a fundamental emotion to a lot of people. But it might also be interpreted as a relic of a particular kind of class anxiety.

Saul Leiter, *Jean,* c. 1948

THE GAME OF ARCANE EMOTIONS

Do you ever have a feeling that you can't quite put a name to? Perhaps it's because you're using the wrong language. Emotions, alongside music and math, are often said to be a universal language of humanity, transcending cultural and linguistic divides, but many languages contain words for emotions that cannot easily be translated.

Can you guess which is the real definition for each of these terms? And do you relate to the experience it describes? Answers are on page 139.

1. TORSCHLUSSPANIK

a)   The agitated feeling that time is running out and possibilities are dwindling.

b)   A sudden dread that you have lost or forgotten something extremely important.

c)   The awful realization that you don't have the knowledge or expertise to deal with a problem or question confronting you.

2. IKTSUARPOK

a)   The blissful release of suddenly realizing that the thing you were worrying about is utterly unimportant.

b)   The sudden urge to commit an act of pointless self-sabotage, such as jumping off a cliff or throwing your phone into a river.

c)   A fidgety anticipation that leaves you unable to focus while waiting for visitors to show up.

3. LITOST

a)   A combination of shame, resentment, and vengeful fury as it dawns on you that you feel utterly wretched and someone else is to blame.

b)   A term for the blend of guilt and irritation you feel on opening an unsuitable or useless gift.

c)   Preemptive regret: for instance, when succumbing to the urge to sleep with your ex or eat a third slice of cake.

4. KOI NO YOKAN

a)   Fear of losing face.

b)   A presentiment of future love on first meeting someone.

c)   The experience of poignant transient beauty that is bound to fade, as with blossoms in springtime.

5. OODAL

a) The thrilled tranquility you experience when you are safe at home in stormy weather.

b) The brand of exaggerated, demonstrative anger that's really a gambit to gain ground in a lovers' tiff.

c) An excess of euphoric energy that, especially in small children, is certain to end in tears.

6. SANKOCH

a) Awkwardness and hesitancy about receiving more than your due—accepting a gift or another helping of food, for instance.

b) A feeling of balance in body and mind: not happiness, exactly, but a sense that everything is as it should be.

c) A sudden apathy about something that you are supposed to be passionate about, often in the middle of an important task or a discussion.

7. HIRAETH

a) A kind of reflectiveness and openness to new thoughts that only happens when you're in transit—for example, while staring out of a train window.

b) The giddy and not unpleasant sensation that comes over you when you notice that you are lost.

c) A fragile, yearning, bittersweet feeling of connection to the landscape of your childhood.

8. FORELSKET

a) The dizzy elation you feel when you first start to fall in love with somebody.

b) A feeling of solidarity with a stranger when you share a slightly awkward moment, such as when your eyes meet after you have spotted them picking their nose.

c) Awe and terror inspired by a natural phenomenon, such as a massive mountain or wild ocean.

9. GIGIL

a) The disconcertingly violent impulse to pinch or squeeze something cute, such as a baby animal.

b) Irritation and dismay at wasted time, as when you wake up after an unintentional afternoon nap.

c) A confusing moment of lust for someone completely unsuitable, whom you would never expect to think of in a romantic or sexual way.

10. MYÖTÄHÄPEÄ

a) Virtuous exhaustion after a day of hard work or intense physical activity.

b) Embarrassment by proxy on witnessing another person's humiliation.

c) A feeling of communion and mutual recognition when you meet the gaze of an animal in its natural environment.

11. GRENG-JAI

a)   The clarity and serenity that comes after cleaning or putting things in order.

b)   A kind of happily unrequited love that you can enjoy precisely because you know that there is no chance of consummation.

c)   An all-consuming dread of putting someone else out or causing them even minor discomfort.

12. MUDITA

a)   Delight at the good fortune or well-being of another person.

b)   The feeling of awkwardness when you start to return to your senses after falling into a rage, as you start to see how unreasonable you've been.

c)   The feeling of mingled awe, pity, and wistfulness that you feel when you glimpse the enormity and interconnectedness of life and the universe.

13. ABBIOCCO

a)   The illicit pleasure of knowing that you've just gotten away with something—maybe after selling something for more than it was really worth.

b)   Drowsiness after eating a big meal, when you're overcome by the need to collapse on the nearest sofa.

c)   A feeling of early-morning alertness and zest for life.

14. ONSRA

a)   A doomed, bittersweet kind of love that you know cannot last.

b)   Guilty resentment and jealousy at the success of a close friend for whom you should be uncomplicatedly happy.

c)   Perverse pride in an ostensibly negative quality or habit (such as being forgetful or habitually late).

15. KAMA MUTA

a)   A sort of grief that expresses itself as a violent and sometimes murderous rage.

b)   Deep love of the intimate, comfortable sort that is only possible between people who have spent much of their lives together.

c)   An ephemeral but overwhelming surge of tender feelings such as love and joy.

ANSWERS

1a

The German word for the agitated, fretful feeling we get when we notice time is running out. Literally translated as "gate-closing panic," *Torschlusspanik* was coined in the Middle Ages to describe the worry of spotting an army rapidly approaching and knowing that the castle gates would not close in time to stop them. A modern-day equivalent that's at least somewhat close to this original meaning appeared in English in 1981, when *Time* magazine reported on a fever of *Torschlusspanik* among East Germans rushing to flee their homes while the borders were still porous enough to escape. But it's more usually used in modern-day German as a metaphor for the feeling that your options in life are becoming restricted—the spark for a midlife crisis, perhaps. German is a rich source of unusually specific and evocative terms for emotional experiences because its convention of splicing words together coins compound nouns. In this way, metaphors that might be expressed in English by a sentence-long idiom become single terms.

2c

That unsettled state of waiting for company, in which we keep glancing out of the window or pause midsentence, thinking we've heard the sound of the car, has a name among the Inuit. More specifically, *iktsuarpok* is the feeling of scanning the endless white horizons of the frozen landscape while waiting for a sled to appear.

3a

Litost is a Czech word that is notoriously hard to translate. The novelist Milan Kundera defines it as "a state of torment caused by a sudden sight of one's misery…like a two-stroke motor. First comes the feeling of torment, then the desire for revenge." He was perplexed by the lack of equivalent terms in other languages and found it "difficult to imagine how anyone can understand the human soul without it."

The most distinctive thing about *litost* is not so much the wretchedness as the fact that the vengeful feelings proceeding from that wretchedness overwhelm any regard for the restoration of your own well-being. A person consumed by *litost* would rather drag others into the gutter than claw their way out of it.

Kundera suggests that some of this feeling might be explained by the fact that much of what is now the Czech Republic has been continually occupied and subjugated throughout its history. *Litost* is the urge for justice as felt by the conquered, the underdog: lacking any hope of pride being restored, all that is left is to use whatever means necessary to wreak misery on the oppressor.

4b

Koi no yokan is not love at first sight; there is a separate Japanese word—*hitomebore*—for that. If anything, the phrase is its more coy and cautious cousin—the premonition of a connection that might be destined to blossom into true love.

In contemporary Japanese culture, *koi no yokan* is a frequent trope in manga comics marketed to teenage girls; it has romantic, almost mystical connotations of shared destiny and the communion of souls. There may always have been some element of this, but the idea might have more practical origins. Traditional Japanese courtships were heavily circumscribed and monitored by the community. Particularly in upper-class families, marriages tended to be arranged and lovers were given limited freedom to express themselves to one another or decide their collective fate. In this environment, perhaps the more tentative *koi no yokan* was the closest a lover could prudently come to expressing ardent emotion.

5b

Tamil has three terms for a lovers' tiff: *oodal*, *pulavi*, and *thuni*. *Oodal* is the least serious of these: it describes the histrionic anger that follows a quarrel, when one person sulks and pouts dramatically to make the other relent and admit their mistake.

Oodal is one of the five canonical themes that structure traditional Tamil songs. In the vast majority of performances, the singer is a woman expressing anger at a transgression by her husband. These songs often insinuate that the small power struggle will be resolved by erotic means. *Oodal* is not entirely negative; it's one thread in the warp and weft of intimacy and a sign that the relationship is grounded in passion and mutual fascination.

6a

Sankoch is used in many Indian languages, not just to suggest hesitation, which is the literal meaning, but for a feeling of embarrassment at the receipt of a gift whose generosity you feel unable to reciprocate.

The significance of the idea of *sankoch* in Indian cultures is probably linked to traditions of hospitality: guests are often lavished with generous gifts and copious amounts of food and feel a growing weight of obligation to return the favor. At such a moment a kind host might urge the guest not to feel *sankochka*, indicating that there is no need to reciprocate in kind.

7c

Hiraeth is a kind of homesickness that is also a longing for some idealized home that may never have truly existed.

This Welsh term has a poetic kinship with the word *saudade*, a sense of melancholy that is supposedly characteristic of the Portuguese or Brazilian temperament. Like *hiraeth*, it evokes wistfulness for a place that never was. But while there might be something universal in this feeling, it's perhaps not surprising that the Welsh, with their history of colonization by the English, harbor this sense of incompleteness or distance pertaining to their homeland. *Hiraeth* is a key part of the living traditions of poetry that are performed at the annual Welsh Eisteddfod.

8a

Forelsket is often said to be an untranslatable Norwegian term for the heady sensations you feel in the first flush of love. Its literal translation, though, is simply "in love." What is different is that Norwegians only tend to apply that term to the dreamy, early-stage feelings of a relationship. Maybe it's an intense crush, maybe it's a once-in-a-millennium romance that will launch moon missions and make empires crumble. What defines being in love is not the intensity but the stage of the affair.

Of course, like all of these definitions, this is probably making things sound neater than they really are. Concepts as abstract and expansive as love are always difficult to pin down, even in your own native language. If we could be sure that everybody meant the same thing when they said "I love you," a lot of relationship anxieties would evaporate in an instant.

9a

"Oh, you're so cute I could just eat you up!" It's not just a melodramatic turn of phrase: the overwhelming surge of affection and protectiveness on encountering a sweet animal or baby is often accompanied by a rush of disturbing hostility. Today this phenomenon is widely recognized; in English it is known as "cute aggression," but only in Tagalog (the language of the Philippines) does it have a name. *Gigil* is the urge to squeeze, pinch, or even bite something you find adorable.

The reason why this affection comes laced with a dash of violence not completely clear, but psychologists have developed some working hypotheses. One is that such robustness regulates the incapacitatingly squishy feelings of tenderness that might otherwise inhibit the alertness necessary for offering protection and care. This is just one example of "dimorphous expression": the activation of an opposing emotional response that acts as a counterweight to an overwhelming feeling. Other instances of dimorphous expression include crying with happiness or the almost angry celebrations that athletes often indulge in after a big win.

Another, more sinister theory is that cute aggression comes from a possessive, acquisitive impulse to lay claim to the object of your affection. If this is true, then when you get the urge to squeeze a sweet baby, there's some part of your primitive brain that actually wants to steal it. Finally, there is an even more disturbing idea that cute aggression arises from an urge to express dominance, strength, and power: rather than stealing the kitten, perhaps what some dark part of us really craves is to eat it up.

10b

A teenager spots their parent flirting with an attractive waiter and turns red with mortification. A sensitive soul watching a comedy is so horrified by the protagonist's lack of self-awareness that they have to switch it off. Often we cringe more at other people's transgressions than at our own.

In Finland, the word for this is *myötähäpeä*: the feeling of vicarious embarrassment when somebody is making a fool of themselves.

11c

In Thailand there is a strong culture of concern for the collective good. The idea of doing or saying something that causes another person discomfort is almost taboo. *Greng-jai* is the dread of putting someone else out or letting them down. There is a trace of this sentiment in the English phrase "I'm *afraid* I can't come to your party."

Thai government and media often locate *greng-jai* as a core element in the national psyche. It's been suggested that this modern idea of exceptional Thai politeness might have something to do with the appalling behavior of Western tourists in Southeast Asia. Witnessing the destructive hedonism of gap-year backpackers and stag partyers, Thai observers not unreasonably conclude that consideration for other people's feelings is not as universal as it ought to be.

Greng-jai also has a secondary meaning: deference to somebody who is older or of higher social rank. Social life in Thailand was traditionally governed by strict social codes operating within a well-defined hierarchy of class, status, and age. In this context, there would be few greater mortifications than realizing that you had caused inconvenience to someone of higher rank.

12a

The German term *schadenfreude* is often gleefully quoted as evidence of the basic meanness of human nature: "There is something in the misfortune of others that does not displease us," as the French writer François de la Rochefoucauld famously said. If you're looking for a more uplifting perspective, try the Buddhist concept of *mudita*: pleasure and delight derived from the well-being of others.

Mudita is one of the four immeasurables or four sublime attitudes that must be cultivated through meditation. In this framework, more elevated emotions are not something that comes naturally, but must be cultivated by mindfulness and conscious habit formation. To begin nurturing *mudita*, the fifth-century scholar Buddhaghosa suggested, focus on someone who is neither a stranger nor an enemy nor a loved one. Instead, think of an acquaintance who seems generally to maintain a cheerful and optimistic attitude. Let your mind rest on their positive outlook and allow it to envelop you.

The next stage is to expand this positive consciousness to others: close family, people toward whom you feel antipathy—and eventually yourself. The goal is to open up your sense of sympathetic joy until it becomes a benevolent attitude to the world in all its multitudinous oneness.

13b

This is what happens when a cuisine endorses a pasta course in addition to starter, entrée, and dessert: *abbiocco* is the overwhelming drowsiness that comes after eating a large Italian meal.

14a

In the Boro language, spoken in parts of India, Nepal, Bhutan, and Bangladesh, *onsra* describes that particular bittersweet love that is colored by a conviction that it cannot last. Perhaps the relationship is nearing its end or the couple is ultimately incompatible, but in the moment the passion is undeniably real.

The poignancy and intensity of a love that cannot last is a trope in all manner of artistic traditions. Doomed lovers litter romantic fiction, from Romeo and Juliet to Bonnie and Clyde. Perhaps this is to do with the inextricable relationship between love and death: the passionate attachment to something in this world heightens the preemptive pain at the loss of it all. Or perhaps, more cynically, it's just easier to maintain a sense of purity in love when there is no prospect of it maturing into bickering over whose fault it is that you're out of toilet paper.

In any case, while the word *onsra* may be unique and untranslatable, the idea can be found worldwide.

15c

Kama is Sanskrit for "love" or "longing." It often has erotic connotations, but it can also refer to the appreciation of aesthetic beauty or any other pleasure deriving from the senses. *Kama muta* is to be briefly but powerfully moved or transported by this feeling of love.

Recently, the term has developed a second life with the help of a group of psychologists and anthropologists who believe that feelings of overwhelming unity and transcendence are a vital, underappreciated element of the human experience. Researchers at the Kama Muta Lab in Oslo have interviewed over 1,000 people in nineteen countries about these experiences and claim to find striking similarities in the package of subjective feelings and physical manifestations. It lasts only briefly and comes with a "sudden intensification of communal sharing—that is, sudden 'love,' or kindness." It is accompanied by warmth in the chest, goosebumps, and a lump in the throat. And it stimulates those who experience it into closer bonds with their companions. This sense of being touched or moved can come from a feeling of oneness with anything from the cosmos to a football team to a kitten.

The Kama Muta Lab researchers believe these feelings could be harnessed to break down barriers within communities and build social harmony. There are plenty of doubts that could be raised about these ideas. Do the researchers really understand the nuances of this term among the cultures where it is used, and can it be successfully translated to others? Can any emotion, fleeting and contingent by nature, really be manufactured to produce long-lasting change? What might be the ethics of manipulating emotion in this way? Despite such questions, it's clear that there is a gap in our language of emotion for terms for experiences that marry communal, convivial sentiments with spiritual and transcendental ones.

"ANGER IS AN ENERGY": FEMINIST ART

NATALIE HUME

John Lydon was right: anger can bring about dramatic change. Both primal and dangerous, its open expression is a preserve of the powerful. While white men have traditionally been granted the privilege to express righteous rage with very little censure, women's anger has been systematically labeled as trivial and pathological. The self-perpetuating logic of power means that their anger is only heard when it is disruptive, reinforcing the stigma that an angry woman is hysterical or mad, incapable of rational thought. This double bind has proved fruitful in the realm of feminist art, where women have found creative and often entertaining ways to expose the rigidness of the sexual hierarchy and to vent their sense of injustice.

The sixteenth-century Italian painter Artemisia Gentileschi has received significant attention in recent years, not only for her vivid dramatization and confident treatment of light and shadow but also for her commitment to representing powerful women protagonists (Gentileschi was a rape survivor). One painting represents the biblical figure Judith with both arms braced, one fist against the head of the Assyrian general Holofernes and the other grasping the sword that slices through his neck, blood snaking down the bed linen. Judith was also among the subjects represented by a younger Italian artist, Elisabetta Sirani, who set up an academy for female artists before her untimely death at twenty-seven. But it is Sirani's Timoclea that stands out for its startling vitality: it portrays the moment when the Theban woman Timoclea overpowers the Thracian soldier who has just raped her, pushing him headfirst into a well, limbs flailing and his face registering shock at his unaccustomed position of helplessness.

With the emergence of performance art, these expressions of anger and rebellion became more playful and experimental. In the early 1960s, the French American artist and former teenage fashion model Niki de Saint Phalle developed her *tirs* (shooting pictures). She would attach bags of colored paint to a large board along with found items such as dolls and kitchen utensils, then cover the whole thing with white plaster. Dressed in a pristine white jumpsuit, she would shoot the paintings with a rifle or pistol, producing a wild mess of paint that mixed and congealed as it slid toward the floor. As well as being a travesty of the precise, planned violence epitomized by the military, the *tirs*, in rejecting pattern and embracing gravity, responded provocatively to Jackson Pollock's intricate (and highly gendered) horizontal drip paintings.

Selma Selman has adapted the practice of Saint Phalle's fellow *nouveau-realiste* Arman, a French American artist who destroyed objects, often musical instruments or valuable items such as cars, by smashing, cutting, and burning. Selman, a Bosnian artist of Roma origin, revels in visiting this violent energy not only upon cars but also upon the apparatus of domestic labor such as washing machines and vacuum cleaners. As well as commenting on gender roles and women's unpaid labor, destroying these mass-produced machines carries a special meaning for Selman, because of her childhood memories of salvaging parts with her father. One day she hopes to destroy a private jet.

La lutte continue.

Niki de Saint Phalle, *Shooting Picture*, 1961

Selma Selman, *Self portrait II*, 2017 (video length: 13' 0"). Photo documentation: Tibor Varga Somogyi. Courtesy of the artist

Professional mourner, ancient Egypt

PROFESSIONAL MOURNERS

A woman sits on a stool staring straight ahead and wailing, racked with rhythmic sobs as tears stream down her cheeks. A few feet away, another is draped head to toe in a long, white veil, which she tears with her hands as she howls a visceral lament. Alongside these spectacles of unfettered grief are other, more formal displays. One man sings stately and forlorn melodies, accompanying himself on an accordion, while a trio of singers chant haunting harmonies in Greek. Each falters at the boundary between singing and sobbing: the keening comes in descending, melodic bursts, lilting and choked. This is a performance of a kind, although the stars are not actors in the conventional sense: they are professional mourners, gathered by the artist Taryn Simon for her 2016 installation *An Occupation of Loss.*

In Western Europe and the United States, lamentations like this are more likely to be encountered on a stage or in an art installation than at a funeral. But ritualized performances of grief are a vital and long-standing element in the funerary customs of cultures all over the world, and often there are individuals whose role is to guide and shape the expression of loss. These professional mourners (or moirologists, as they are technically called) may not be intimately acquainted with the deceased person, yet it falls on them to express a collective sense of sorrow and despair that is no less authentic for its formal and deliberate nature.

The role played by professional mourners varies from one culture to another. In some traditions, designated mourners offer a model, giving form to the amorphous void of grief. In Azerbaijan, mourning women chant, sway, and slap their palms against their legs while wailing; gradually, the collected family and friends join the motion and enter into this trancelike enactment of grief. Funeral chanters in Ecuador, inheritors of indigenous traditions that predate the European arrival in the Americas, are treated with suspicion because of the depth of feeling they might elicit (they have been said to provoke fainting and even suicide). In Ghana, family networks often include a dirge singer or wailer; if not, the bereaved may recruit one from elsewhere. These women, versed in a form of emotional experience for which everyday vocabulary is insufficient, demonstrate an expression of grief for others to follow. The Yezidis of Armenia have an entire mode of communication used only for discussing trauma, suffering, and loss: melodized speaking, which lies somewhere between singing and talking, is used by performers at funerals but also in everyday conversation when the topics become too painful for ordinary words.

In other cultures, theaters of sorrow serve not as exemplars but as counterpoints to the stoicism expected of the bereaved. In Northern Albania, for instance, the parents of a dead child are traditionally expected to suppress tears and harden themselves against any visible sign of grief. Their "uncried words" are transformed into ritual wailing. Women's laments are called the "wailing of milk," while men's are the "wailing of blood." Elsewhere, the divide is even more gendered: in Dagestan in Russia, only men are allowed to stand near the coffin, and for them tears are taboo. Women follow at a distance, weeping profusely.

In most cases, these customs are thousands of years old, predating the advent of Christianity or Islam. During ancient Egyptian funerals, women were employed to enact inconsolable grief. This was a sacred role that came with high status but stringent demands: such women were expected to shave their heads and forgo the privilege of having children. In China, professional mourning has existed as a vocation for around 2,000 years. Today, it survives not only as a remnant of an ancient tradition but as a modern industry, with agencies hiring out mourners and especially high rates paid to those who can weep convincingly on demand.

Traditions of lamentation that survive in parts of Greece can be traced back to Sophocles, who depicted two mourners chanting a harmonic dirge while the third sings a more free-flowing improvisation inspired by birdsong. The British writer Patrick Leigh Fermor became fascinated by the ability of certain women in the Mani Peninsula to improvise elaborate poems at local funerals, singing them while weeping in a meter which, he believed, had no relation to any other musical form. He found this ritual "hysteria" healthier and more honest than the "decorous little services of the West, the hushed voices, the self-control, our brave smiles and calmness."

But what Fermor called the West has related traditions of its own. Evidence of ritualized mourning practices in medieval Europe survives in the shape of *pleurants* or weepers, adorning noble tombs. These rituals may have taken influence from a tantalizing passage in the Bible: "Feign thyself to be a mourner, and put on now mourning apparel" (2 Samuel 14:2). The still and silent statues presage a more recent tradition of professional mourning in Western Europe: funeral mutes, commonplace in the eighteenth and nineteenth centuries, were employed to stand sentry outside the houses of the recently deceased or to trudge alongside hearses. They offered no eloquent lamentations or primal wails but maintained an austere silence, a blankness echoed by their clothes: black cloaks, black hats, a long black stick draped in black material. This pantomime of stoical sorrow often provoked ridicule rather than respect, as in the case of Charles Dickens's Oliver Twist, the most famous of funeral mutes. By the nineteenth century, mutes were regularly portrayed as disreputable urchins, profiting from other people's misery and hiding bottles of spirits beneath their cloaks. As a cartoon published in an 1891 *Punch* article had it:

And yet to my mem'ry he'll never appear
A compound delightful of sorrow and beer.
He was paid to look wretched and can't be rebuked,
The more money he got the more wretched he looked.

The cynicism expressed in poems like this—the suspicions of insincerity, the distaste at profiting from other people's loss—proved fatal to the tradition of funeral mutes, and in Europe and America professional mourning has remained unfashionable ever since. When in 2013 a British firm was inspired by foreign examples to start offering the services of paid mourners, they found that the demand was lacking and closed within a few years. Similar anxieties exist in cultures that retain traditions of professional mourning. Often women hired to mourn are poor and of low status, equated with sex workers and stigmatized in a similar way. As in ancient Egypt, death and sex are intimately and uncomfortably linked. Yet in all these cultures, designated mourners have nevertheless had a vital place in funeral customs, helping to give shape to emotional experiences that cannot be contained by standard emotional vocabulary. What is more, there is no question in the minds of professional mourners that the emotions they express are authentic and real. When the performers in *An Occupation of Loss* were asked how they mimic the behavior of a bereaved person, every one of them agreed that the role could only be performed by summoning the emotion they were expected to convey.

Helen Macdonald in her grief memoir *H Is for Hawk* writes that "shocking loss isn't to be shared, no matter how hard you try." A century and a half earlier, Elizabeth Barrett Browning's poem "Grief" displayed a similar conviction that the deepest sorrow is internal and incommunicable:

Deep-hearted man, express
Grief for thy dead in silence like to death—
Most like a monumental statue set
In everlasting watch and moveless woe
Till itself crumble to the dust beneath.
Touch it; the marble eyelids are not wet:
If it could weep, it could arise and go.

The silent, motionless grief this describes is surely the same emotion as the one embodied by those funeral mutes, one of many ways in which the emotions of loss can be embodied and brought into the social world.

Unknown photographer, holy fakir, India, 19th century

5

TRANSCENDENCE

TARANTISM

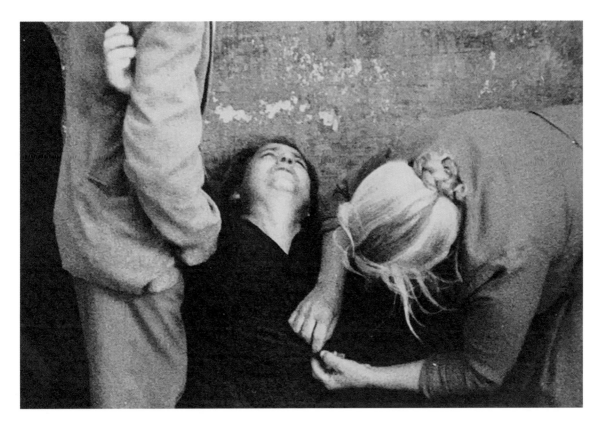

The people in these photos, taken by an unknown photographer in 1958 in Galatina, are victims of tarantism, a kind of pathological frenzy peculiar to Italy. The condition was traditionally thought to be induced by the bite of the wolf spider, causing a sort of possession: "When one is in the hold of this ill-wished beast," wrote the eighteenth-century physician Nicola Caputo, "one has a hundred different feelings at a time. One cries, dances, vomits, trembles, laughs, pales, cries, faints, and one will suffer great pain, and finally after a few days, if unaided, you die."

Wild, frantic dancing is both a symptom of tarantism and its only cure. Those afflicted often have an uncontrollable desire to dance, and folk wisdom advocates indulging this urge. Caputo recounts a story about a peasant woman in Lecce who was brought into town in a stupor after a suspected spider bite. Musicians were summoned and brought violins and tambourines to play a lively *pizzica pizzica*. At first, the woman did not respond. But then, Caputo writes:

At the third melody, or maybe the fourth, the young woman in my presence awoke and began to dance with so much force and fury that one might have called her crazy....After two days of dance, she was free and healed.

This is the origin of the tarantella, a dance that is a key part of Henrik Ibsen's 1879 play *A Doll's House*.

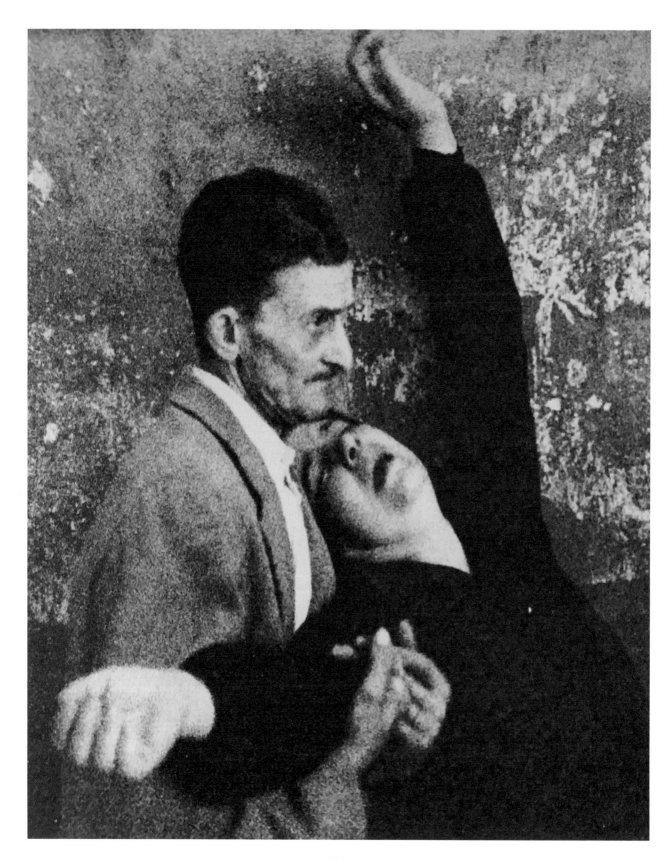

ECSTASY JULES EVANS

When I was twenty-four I had a near-death experience immediately after a skiing accident. I fell off a cliff, broke my leg, and was instantly transported to a different "place," where I was immersed in white light and felt full of love. It was impossible to describe or comprehend, yet it was profoundly healing and life-altering. It felt like an experience of ecstasy.

Today the common understanding of the word "ecstatic" is either "extremely happy" or a reference to the drug MDMA. But the word has a much older meaning, from the Ancient Greek *ekstasis*, meaning "standing outside." In this original sense, ecstasy is a moment when you stand outside, or go beyond, your ordinary sense of self. In ancient Greek culture, it was often connected with the experience of *enthousiasmos*, or "having a god within"—from which we get the modern word "enthusiasm." An ecstatic experience, then, is a moment when your ordinary sense of self departs or dissolves, and in its place another consciousness—possibly divine—arises.

This sort of ecstatic experience could be exhilarating and empowering—think of the disciples of Jesus being filled with the Holy Spirit at Pentecost, and being granted charismatic gifts such as prophecy and healing. But it could also be terrifying—think of King Pentheus, the hero of Euripides's *Bacchae*, who tries to imprison Dionysus, god of ecstasy, and is instead sent mad by him and torn to shreds.

Most cultures throughout history have had ecstatic rituals, places where people could go to "unself." Ecstatic experiences were understood to be risky, but they had important social functions. First, they helped people to heal from emotional or physical problems. That's still the case today: the founder of Alcoholics Anonymous, Bill Wilson, was freed from his alcoholism after an ecstatic experience, and AA tries to guide addicts to similar liberation through "surrendering to a higher power." Second, they helped connect people: the intense bonding experience of a modern music festival is not unlike ecstatic elements in historical experiences of hunting and war. The sociologist Émile Durkheim thought all cultures needed moments of "collective effervescence" to fuse together. Third, ecstatic experiences give people a sense of meaning in the face of the vastness of the universe and the transience of life. In the ancient Greek ecstatic cult of Eleusis, initiates felt reborn as children of the divine, which meant they could "die with a better hope." Today, scientists are researching how magic mushrooms reduce the fear of death in people with terminal cancer, by giving them an ecstatic sense of connection to the universe.

Finally, ecstatic experiences are simply fun. It's boring to be always stuck in our lonely and self-critical egos. That's why we yearn for occasional "holidays from the self," as Aldous Huxley called them. Humans need occasional ecstasy to get out of our heads, turn off the chatter in our minds, and feel briefly liberated from the ingrained inhibitions of civilization. We're not the only animal that seeks intoxication—moose get drunk on fermented apples, for example, and dolphins get high on puffer fish.

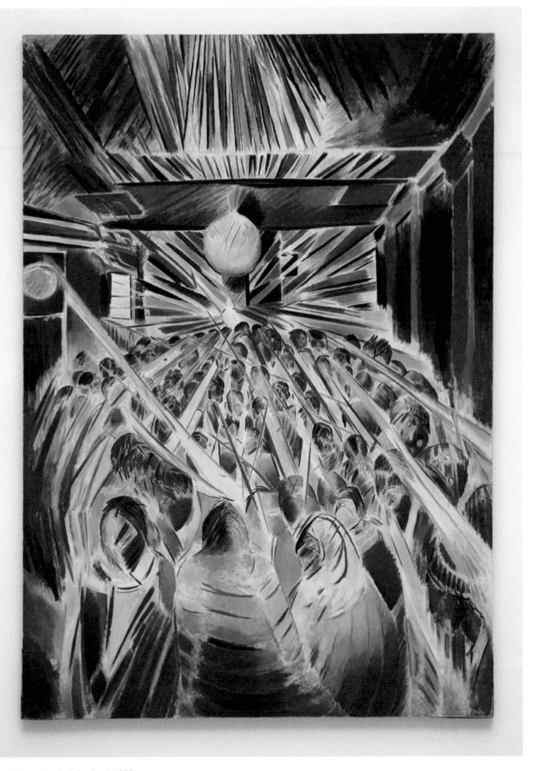

Denzil Forrester, *Dub Strobe 1*, 1990

Photograph by Pipilotti Rist, 2020

While most cultures have recognized ecstatic rituals, Western culture has a problematic relationship to ecstasy. During the seventeenth-century scientific revolution, ecstasy began to be marginalized and pathologized as "enthusiasm," which came to mean an overexcited and delusional frame of mind. Thomas Hobbes, Adam Smith and other secular Enlightenment philosophers blamed this mood for fomenting the Thirty Years' War. The ideal Enlightenment society, they suggested, should be sober, rational, self-controlled, industrious, and entirely free of religious ecstasy. At around the same time, the Anglican and Catholic churches marginalized or banned ecstatic forms of worship. Then, in the late nineteenth century, psychiatrists including Henry Maudsley proposed that religious ecstasy was a symptom of brain disease, perhaps requiring enforced hospitalization.

Gradually, ecstasy had shifted from being a dangerous but meaningful experience to something shameful and suspicious, indicative of stupidity or madness and requiring to be hidden. Nonetheless, ecstatic experiences offer a necessary glimpse beyond the fiction of our everyday selves, and if societies close one avenue for such experiences, people will find another.

Sure enough, over the last two centuries, Western culture has improvised new forms for ecstatic experiences. Romanticism, which the English critic T. E. Hulme described as "spilt religion," was (or is) a cultural movement that found a positive place for ecstasy, which was seen as central to creative inspiration and part of the sensitive human's encounter with the sublime. Mesmerism (an early form of hypnosis) and Spiritualism, which emerged in the nineteenth century, offered new contexts and meanings for ecstatic experiences, with séances being a favorite after-dinner entertainment of many, including Sherlock Holmes creator Arthur Conan Doyle and Queen Victoria. Ecstatic Christianity attracted millions of followers, mainly to Methodism in the eighteenth century or to Pentecostalism in the twentieth century. Today, 35,000 people convert to Pentecostalism every day worldwide.

The 1960s witnessed an explosive renaissance of ecstatic practices, from Buddhist or Hindu meditation and psychedelics to rock and roll and the sexual revolution. A generation followed the musician John Lennon's advice to "turn off your mind, relax, and float downstream." The Harvard psychologist Timothy Leary called for a "neo-ecstatic society," in which everyone would "turn on, tune in, and drop out." President Richard Nixon declared him the most dangerous man in America.

Today, the pursuit of ecstatic experiences is more accepted, whether through psychedelics, sex, dance, prayer and meditation, extreme sports, or gaming and virtual reality. The "ecstatic economy" offers us many ways to take holidays from the self. Yet we still don't really have recognized rituals for ecstatic experiences. Raves, yes, but not rituals. As psychedelic therapies are becoming legalized and being applied to problems such as addiction, trauma, and depression, the scientists developing these treatments are facing interesting research questions. What kind of ecstatic rituals work best for secular Westerners? To what extent should therapists guide people's experiences and interpretations? And what—or whom—do people meet when they go out of their heads?

We are rightly wary of ecstatic experiences. But there is also a risk of ignoring the ecstatic altogether and having no approved places to unself. People will always seek self-transcendence, and if societies don't offer them healthy routes to it, they will find other, riskier avenues.

GODS OF LOVE AND LUST

Deities of love and lust appear in numerous guises across a range of traditions, reflecting the many faces of passion. The list here is far from exhaustive but gives a sense of the emotional range found in personifications of love.

Rāgarāja: the Love-Stained Wisdom King

Rāgarāja (also Aizen Myō-ō) is an Indian god of lust, with an inflamed and slightly obscene appearance—ruddy and grinning. He was originally a Hindu deity but is now more important in the traditions of Buddhism sometimes grouped together as Esoteric, which emphasise arcane knowledge based on alleged secret teachings of Buddha.

Despite Rāgarāja's bawdy, angry appearance and his identification with an uncontrollable, worldly desire, his lust can also be transformed into spiritual awakening. Hence his evocative nickname—the Love-Stained Wisdom King.

Today, he is particularly venerated by sex workers and members of the LGBT community.

Freyja/Freyr

Freyja (or Frigg) is a goddess of fertility and beauty but also of war. She rides a chariot pulled by cats and is accompanied by a wild boar.

Loki mocks her for her promiscuity, claiming that she's slept with every one of the male gods; she's also one of the most powerful and knowledgeable deities in the Norse canon. As a practitioner of *seidr* (a particularly potent form of magic or witchcraft) she posed a threat even to her fellow gods—including Loki, following his taunt.

Freyja's belligerent nature was balanced by tenderness: she wanders the world weeping tears of gold for her absent husband Odr, a god of divine madness and anger. Christian commentators in the nineteenth century tended to emphasise this pining wife figure over the more assertive side of her character.

Freyr was the Norse god of virility, as well as of kingship, harvest, and peace and prosperity, and, like the Egyptian god Min, he is often portrayed with a giant erection. A Norse poem describes him as "the foremost of the gods," "hated by none."

The Buddhist king of passion, Rāgarāja (Aizen Myō-ō), Japan, Edo period, c. 1600–1700

Tu'er Shen

In ancient China, the story goes, a man named Tu'er Shen became infatuated with an anticorruption official who was conducting investigations in his town. He started going out of his way to attend public hearings and followed him on his inspections, just to be in his presence. One day the lovesick man finally confessed his feelings to the object of his devotion. Unfortunately, the inspector did not reciprocate; in fact, he was horrified and murdered his admirer on the spot.

Having witnessed Tu'er Shen's murder, the gods recognized that there were many people in similar situations who needed protection. Tu'er Shen was made into a deity and assigned the duty of defending those who love people of their own gender.

Tu'er Shen's attraction to his own gender hardly marks him out among the indiscriminately licentious gods: there are examples of gay love, or at least lust, in almost every classical mythology. But Tu'er Shen is unusual for this being his defining quality and the cause of his divinity.

Oshun

This goddess, associated with sensuality, water, love, and fertility, is one of the most powerful deities of the Yoruba people of Nigeria. She has also been adopted into Santería, a religious tradition that emerged in Cuba during the era of slavery and combining Yoruba and Catholic beliefs.

Oshun is the giver of life, bestowing sweet waters that make the land bloom; she can also cause destruction, through droughts and floods. In a similar way, she is involved in love's disappointment and failure as well as its consummation.

Egyptian love deities: Hathor, Min, and Qetesh

Hathor, often treated of the mother of the gods, is a famous Egyptian deity strongly associated with love and sexuality—although her many attributes make her much more complex than just a goddess of love.

Min, the most unambiguously sexual (and even kinky) of the gods, is usually represented as a man with a giant erection and holding a whip. Like most gods of love and sex, he is a bringer of fertility and abundance—worshippers prayed that he would confer his fecundity upon crops.

Meanwhile, Qetesh, identified by her lotus flower and serpent, was the goddess of ecstasy, both sacred and sexual.

Tlazoltéotl, queen of filth

This Aztec goddess carries a heady combination of associations: love, purification, steam baths, lust, and filth.

She has four aspects at different stages of her life. First, a freewheeling seductress, and second, a destructive goddess of uncertainty, connected to gambling and peril. In middle age, she is personified as the eater of filth and sin, before finally becoming the terrifying goddess of destruction, especially of young men. In the first two guises, she can provoke sexual vice and iniquity, yet in the third she offers the only means to absolution: she both creates impure behavior and cleanses it.

Inanna/Ishtar/Astarte: forerunner of all love goddesses

The Sumerian goddess Inanna has a claim to being the mother of all goddesses of love. In various guises she appears in ancient civilizations across the Middle East, Europe, and North Africa: Assyrian, Babylonian, Phoenician, Egyptian.

Her nature is not that of the other most prominent female deity, the nurturing mother goddess: she is powerful, impulsive, and assertive. She sometimes exhibits kindness and generosity to humans but can also be vengeful, and she is always her own priority. Perhaps because of her sensuality and independence, she appears frequently in the Old Testament as a hate figure—she's thought to be the idol to whom the Canaanites would burn offerings. Both sides of her character are present in the *Epic of Gilgamesh*: she feuds with the hero for rejecting her advances but later comes to his aid.

Inanna's many names and iterations include the well-known deities Ishtar and Astarte, but she is also thought to be the model for the most famous love goddesses of all: the Greek Aphrodite and her Roman equivalent, Venus. She still watches over us today—tradition has it that she is manifest in the Morning Star.

Mary Bishop, *Untitled* (A woman with a weight attached to her neck prepares to throw herself into the sea), Netherne Hospital, 1960s

OUR LADY OF DARKNESS

In Thomas de Quincey's luridly gothic and luxuriantly miserable prose poem "Levana and Our Ladies of Sorrow," the varieties of emotional suffering are made manifest in the person of three "awful sisters." Each is a servant of Levana, the Roman goddess of childbirth, who charges them with "educating" the innocent by a series of unbearable trials.

The first of the sisters is "Mater Lachrymarum, Our Lady of Tears," whose "eyes are sweet and subtle, wild and sleepy, by turns" and who accompanies mourners in their "raves and moans." The second sister, "Mater Suspirorum, Our Lady of Sighs," neither cries nor moans, but only "weeps inaudibly." She is the constant companion of pariahs and outcasts. It is the third who is most worthy of reverence and dread:

But the third sister, who is also the youngest—! Hush, whisper whilst we talk of her! Her kingdom is not large, or else no flesh should live; but within that kingdom all power is hers. Her head, turreted like that of Cybèle, rises almost beyond the reach of sight. She droops not; and her eyes rising so high might be hidden by distance; but, being what they are, they cannot be hidden; through the treble veil of crape which she wears, the fierce light of a blazing misery, that rests not for matins or for vespers, for noon of day or noon of night, for ebbing or for flowing tide, may be read from the very ground. She is the defier of God. She is also the mother of lunacies, and the suggestress of suicides. Deep lie the roots of her power; but narrow is the nation that she rules. For she can approach only those in whom a profound nature has been upheaved by central convulsions; in whom the heart trembles, and the brain rocks under conspiracies of tempest from without and tempest from within. Madonna moves with uncertain steps, fast or slow, but still with tragic grace. Our Lady of Sighs creeps timidly and stealthily. But this youngest sister moves with incalculable motions, bounding, and with tiger's leaps. She carries no key; for, though coming rarely amongst men, she storms all doors at which she is permitted to enter at all. And her name is Mater Tenebrarum—Our Lady of Darkness.

ON HAPPINESS

GIROLAMO CARDANO

Let us live, therefore, cheerfully, although there be no lasting joy in mortal things, whose substance is evanescent, inane, and vacuous. But if there is any good thing by which you would adorn this stage of life, we have not of such been cheated—rest, serenity, modesty, self-restraint, orderliness, change, fun, entertainment, society, temperance, sleep, food, drink, riding, sailing, walking, keeping abreast of events, meditation, contemplation, education, piety, marriage, feasting, the satisfaction of recalling an orderly disposition of the past, cleanliness, water, fire, listening to music, looking at all about one, talks, stories, history, liberty, continence, little birds, puppies, cats, consolation of death, and the common flux of time, fate and fortune, over the afflicted and the favored alike. There is a good hope for things beyond all hope; good in the exercise of some art in which one is skilled; good in meditating upon the manifold transmutation of all nature and upon the magnitude of Earth.

Italy, 1501

WILLA CATHER

The earth was warm under me, and warm as I crumbled it through my fingers. Queer little red bugs came out and moved in slow squadrons around me. Their backs were polished vermilion, with black spots. I kept as still as I could. Nothing happened. I did not expect anything to happen. I was something that lay under the sun and felt it, like the pumpkins, and I did not want to be anything more. I was entirely happy. Perhaps we feel like that when we die and become a part of something entire, whether it is sun and air, or goodness and knowledge. At any rate, that is happiness; to be dissolved into something complete and great. When it comes to one, it comes as naturally as sleep.

From Willa Cather, *My Antonia*, 1918

ÉMILIE DU CHÂTELET

It is commonly believed that it is difficult to be happy, and there is much reason for such a belief; but it would be much easier for men to be happy if reflecting on and planning conduct preceded action. One is carried along by circumstances and indulges in hopes that never yield half of what one expects. Finally, one clearly perceives the means to be happy only when age and self-imposed fetters put obstacles in one's way.

Let us anticipate the reflections that we make too late: those who will read these pages will find what age and the circumstances of their life would provide too slowly. Let us prevent readers from losing a part of the precious short time that all of us have to feel and to think; and from giving their time to caulking their ship, time which they should devote to securing the pleasures that they can enjoy on their voyage.

In order to be happy, one must have freed oneself of prejudices, one must be virtuous, healthy, have tastes and passions, and be susceptible to illusions; for we owe most of our pleasures to illusions, and unhappy is the one who has lost them. Far then, from seeking to make them disappear by the torch of reason, let us try to thicken the varnish that illusion lays on the majority of objects. It is even more necessary to them than are care and finery to our body.

One must begin by saying to oneself, and by convincing oneself, that we have nothing to do in the world but to obtain for ourselves some agreeable sensations and feelings. The moralists who say to men, curb your passions and master your desires if you want to be happy, do not know the route to happiness. One is only happy because of satisfied tastes and passions, and lacking passions, one must be content with tastes.

***

...So let us try to be healthy, to have no prejudices, to have passions, to make them serve our happiness, to replace our passions with inclinations, to cherish our illusions, to be virtuous, never to repent, to keep away from sad ideas, and never allow our heart to sustain a spark of inclination for someone whose inclination for us diminishes and who ceases to love us. We must leave love behind one day, if we do indeed age, and that day must be the one when love ceases to make us happy. Lastly, let us think of fostering a taste for study, a taste which makes our happiness depend only on ourselves. Let us preserve ourselves from ambition, and, above all, let us be certain of what we want to be; let us choose for ourselves our path in life, and let us try to strew that path with flowers.

From *The Art of Happiness: The Reflections of Émilie Du Châtelet*, 1746, translated by Judith P. Zinsser and Isabelle Bour

CODA: EMOTIONAL ACTIVITIES AND GAMES

Emotional charades

Write a selection of actions on pieces of paper and place them into a bag. For instance: eating a sandwich, playing badminton, scratching your head. Then write a selection of emotional states—such as smug, defiant, adoring—and place them in a separate bag. Take turns in removing one word from each bag and carrying out the action in the style of the emotion: smugly eating a sandwich or defiantly scratching your head. The first player to guess the emotion being performed gets a point, then words rotate to the next player.

The laughing bug

We tend to think that laughter is a response to humor, but studies of monitoring people's laughter suggest that it's more like a social contagion than an appraisal of wit: by far the most reliable trigger for laughter is other people laughing. That's why comedy shows often use laugh tracks and why one of the earliest hit records was the 1918 "Okeh laughing tape," which consists of almost nothing except the sound of two people guffawing uncontrollably. You can try it yourself: gather a group of people and simultaneously begin to mimic a laugh. Keep going, and at some point, your laughter will almost certainly cease to be fake. It doesn't work if you're alone!

Emotional recall

This is a key element of the Stanislavski method, in which actors seek to bring truth to the performance by experiencing their character's mental state as fully as possible. To practice emotional recall, pick a feeling. Start with a positive one such as joy—going too deep into a darker emotion carries some obvious risks. Hold the memory in your mind as clearly as possible and write down every detail you can recall: what you could see, hear, smell, what your body felt like and what thoughts passed through your head. Can you reawaken the feeling as though it were the first time?

The "I feel" game

Find a partner and look into each others' eyes. Take turns making a statement; each one must begin with the words "I feel." You might start simple—such as "I feel awkward" or "I feel a bit cold"—but as you go on, the emotions you express are likely to get more complicated. You can say how you feel about the statement your partner has just made, for instance, or how you feel about playing this game. You must continue for at least three minutes, beginning every statement with "I feel." You might be surprised what emotions get unearthed.

Emotions without labels

Sit down in a comfortable place, close your eyes, and focus on your breathing. Now pay attention to what's going on in your body and mind. Instead of reaching for a label, try instead to describe it in terms of physical sensations: what parts of your body feel hot or cold, tight or relaxed? Write down how you feel you in as much detail as possible without using an emotion adjective such as "anxious" or "content."

Make your own emotion

In Douglas Adams's *The Meaning of Liff*, a "dictionary of things that there aren't any words for yet," each definition is assigned to the name of a place. Try this with emotions. Using an atlas (or Google Maps), pick a random city. Now assign that city a definition that describes an emotion you have experienced but never found a word for. An example from Douglas Adams: "GLASGOW (n.) The feeling of infinite sadness engendered when walking through a place filled with happy people fifteen years younger than yourself." If you are playing in a group, you can make it competitive by voting on which word should be brought into common usage.

FURTHER READING

Ahmed, Sara. *The Cultural Politics of Emotion*. Routledge, 2004.

Arikha, Noga. *Passions and Tempers: A History of the Humours*. Ecco, 2008.

Black, Margaret J., and Stephen A. Mitchell. *Freud and Beyond: A History of Modern Psychoanalytic Thought*. Basic Books, 1996.

Bourke, Joanna. *Fear: A Cultural History*. Virago, 2005.

Burton, Robert. *The Anatomy of Melancholy*. Penguin, 2002. First published 1621.

Damasio, Antonio. *The Feeling of What Happens: Body, Emotion and the Making of Consciousness*. Vintage, 2000.

Darwin, Charles. *The Expression of the Emotions in Man and Animals*. Penguin, 2009. First published 1872.

Davies, William. *The Happiness Industry: How the Government and Big Business Sold Us Well-Being*. Verso, 2016.

Dixon, Thomas. *From Passions to Emotions: The Creation of a Secular Psychological Category*. Cambridge Unversity Press, 2003.

Ekman, Paul. *Emotions Revealed: Recognising Faces and Feelings to Improve Communication and Emotional Life*. Holt, 2007.

Evans, Jules. *The Art of Losing Control: A Philosopher's Search for Ecstatic Experience*. Canongate, 2017.

Feldman Barrett, Lisa. *How Emotions Are Made: The Secret Life of the Brain*. Macmillan, 2017.

Frosh, Stephen. *Feelings*. Routledge, 2011.

Goldie, Peter. *The Mess Inside: Narrative, Emotion, and the Mind*. Oxford University Press, 2012.

Hochschild, Arlie. *The Managed Heart: Commercialization of Human Feeling*. University of California Press, 2012.

Huxley, Aldous. *Moksha: Aldous Huxley's Classic Writings on Psychedelics and the Visionary Experience*. Park Street Press, 1999.

James, William. *The Principles of Psychology*. Dover, 2000. First published 1890.

———. *The Varieties of Religious Experience*. Penguin, 1982. First published 1902.

Klein, Melanie. *Envy and Gratitude, and Other Works 1946–1963*. Hogarth Press, 1984.

Mishra, Pankaj, *Age of Anger: A History of the Present*. Allen Lane, 2017.

Ngai, Sianne. *Ugly Feelings*. Harvard University Press, 2017.

Nussbaum, Martha C. *Political Emotions: Why Love Matters for Justice*. Harvard University Press, 2015.

Panksepp, Jaak. *The Archaeology of Mind: Neuroevolutionary Origins of Human Emotions*. Norton, 2012.

Reddy, William. *The Navigation of Feeling: A Framework for the History of Emotions*. Cambridge University Press, 2001.

Ricks, Christopher. *Keats and Embarrassment*. Oxford University Press, 1984.

Robinson, Jack, and Natalia Zagórska-Thomas. *Blush*. CB Editions, 2018.

Solomon, Robert. *Emotions in Asian Thought: A Dialogue in Comparative Philosophy*. State University of New York Press, 1994.

———. *The Passions: Emotions and the Meaning of Life*. Hackett, 1993.

Watt Smith, Tiffany. *The Book of Human Emotions: From Ambiguphobia to Umpty—154 Words from Around the World for How We Feel*. Wellcome, 2016.

Williams, Raymond. *Structures of Feeling: Affectivity and the Study of Culture*. Cambridge University Press, 2001.

Winnicott, D. W. *Playing and Reality*. Tavistock, 1971.

ACKNOWLEDGMENTS

Many people have helped in the creation of this book, emotionally and otherwise.
Among them, special thanks to: Phoebe Arnold, Rose Dempsey, Thomas Dixon,
Margit Erb, Sean French, Nicci Gerrard, Mel Gooding, Leo Hollis, Natalie Hume,
Hiang Kee, Ella Rothenstein, Rob Shaeffer, Tiffany Watt-Smith,
and everybody at the Centre for the History of Emotions.

EDGAR GERRARD HUGHES is a researcher at the Queen Mary Centre for the History of the Emotions in London. He has a PhD in the politics of grief in nineteenth-century Britain.

MARINA WARNER is a novelist, critic, and cultural historian whose wide-ranging works of fiction and nonfiction focus on myths and fairy tales. She has been awarded the British Academy Medal and has been shortlisted for the Booker Prize for Fiction. Her latest book is *Inventory of a Life Mislaid: An Unreliable Memoir*.